A Passion for Patchwork

Over 100 quilted projects for all seasons

A Passion
for Patchwork

Over 100 quilted projects for all seasons

Lise Bergene

D&C
David and Charles

Copyright © Cappelen 2002, 2003, 2004
Originally published in Norway as *Lapper Stort og Smått*
Lappergaver
Julens Lappebok

First published in the UK in 2005 by David & Charles
Brunel House   Newton Abbot   Devon
www.davidandcharles.co.uk
David & Charles is a subsidiary of F+W (UK) Ltd.,
an F+W Publications Inc. company
Reprinted 2005, 2006, 2007
A catalogue record for this book is available from the
British Library.

ISBN 0 7153 2288 5

Paperback edition published in North America in 2005
by KP Books, an F+W Publications Inc. company
700 East State Street, Iola, WI 54990
715-445-2214/888-457-2873
www.krause.com

A catalog record for this book is available from the Library
of Congress: 2005928835

ISBN 0-89689-255-7

Printed in China by R.R. Donnelley

Contents

Before You Start...

The projects in this book use basic fabrics and threads, mostly cotton, and simple patchwork, appliqué and quilting techniques, with the techniques required described within the projects.

Fabrics

It is best to wash all fabrics before use, to rinse out any superfluous colour and additives. Most of the fabrics I use in patchwork are cotton, but it is quite possible to use other types of fabrics, such as linen, silk, wool and synthetic varieties. Consider the area of use for your patchwork quilt when deciding on the fabric. Will it be a wall hanging purely for decoration or is it intended to warm cold knees? If it requires washing once in a while, make sure to choose a fabric that will wash and wear well.

Many quilters feel uncertain about choosing fabric types and colours and most would like to know more about using colours but feel there is too much to learn. Most of us know the simple Log Cabin technique, in which one side is dark and the other light and where colour choice is less important. This principle can be transferred to other patchwork blocks. My advice is: mix the colours you think look good together, but use both light and dark colours for a good result. The designs in this book should give you plenty of inspiration.

Threads

There are many wonderful threads on the market, both for sewing together, quilting and appliqué embroidery. For sewing together, I prefer cotton thread. For quilting and appliqué, I test different threads and see what looks best. Look in your local needlecraft store and magazines for ideas.

Batting (wadding)

There are many different types of batting (wadding) on the market: some are more suited to hand quilting, while others are best for machine quilting. Try out the different types and decide which one you like best. I mostly use pure cotton batting, but you could also use wool batting, synthetic types or cotton/polyester batting.

Measurements

The projects in this book have been stitched using imperial measurements but as some people prefer using metric, inches have been converted to centimetres – but please be aware that these conversions can never be fully accurate. Unless stated otherwise, the seam allowance on all measurements (before sewing together) is ¼in (0.7cm).

Quilting

Patchwork can be quilted in a variety of ways. You can quilt by hand, using a frame or without one, using regular quilt stitches or a series of different embroidery stitches. If machine quilting, you have a number of choices. You can quilt free motion (by lowering the feed dog), using a darning foot and moving the fabric yourself, or quilt with a straight seam or other pattern seams, in which you use an upper feed dog. I enjoy machine quilting the most, because it allows for the most creativity.

Quilting involves working on several layers of fabric and if these layers are not stabilized together you may end up with puckers in your work. To avoid this make a quilt 'sandwich' from the layers of patchwork, batting (wadding) and backing fabric before you start quilting, by tacking (basting) or safety pinning the layers together.

Appliqué with double-sided fusible interfacing

Double-sided fusible interfacing allows you to attach one fabric to another, which makes it ideal for appliqué. You can sew on interfacing appliqués either by hand or with your sewing machine, using a range of stitches and thread.

- Trace the design on to the paper side of the interfacing and cut out the design.
- Iron on the piece of double-sided fusible interfacing, making sure that the adhesive side is facing the wrong side of the fabric.
- Cut out the design and tear off the interfacing paper.
- Iron the cut-out design on to the material, with the adhesive side facing the fabric.
- Finally, appliqué the design on to the fabric by hand or machine.

Frayed-Edge Denim

This technique will allow you to create something original and trendy from an old pair of jeans. You can use it to sew bags, rucksacks, spectacle and mobile phone glasses, small and large bags, pot holders, make-up bags or sewing accessories. The technique is simple: make sure all the seam allowances face the right side and cut notches into them. Machine wash the item, which will make the seam allowance fray.

Stitch as follows for frayed-edge technique:
- Place a piece of denim and another piece of fabric together, wrong sides together.
- Draw up the lines you want to quilt on the piece of denim.
- Fold aside the piece of denim, lay on a piece of batting (wadding) that is smaller than the denim and the batting pieces on to the centre of the piece of fabric; fold back the denim patch over the batting and fabric.
- Pin together the three layers: denim, batting and fabric and machine quilt along the lines you have drawn.
- When sewing together denim with the frayed-edge technique, use a seam allowance of ½in (1.25cm).
- When the model is finished, cut notches into the seam allowances, at intervals of about ½in (1.25cm).
- Finally, machine wash the model at 40°C. Wash blankets and so on in a duvet cover with its opening sewed together, otherwise the loose threads may block your washing machine's drain. The models turn out even better if you tumble dry them.

Denim Pot Holders

These charming pot holders are nice and thick, consisting of a double layer of denim, two layers of cotton fabric and two layers of batting (wadding). You will therefore have to sew two blocks with frayed edges and sew two together to a pot holder.

Stitch as follows for two pot holders:
- Cut out four squares, 7½in (19cm) in denim.
- Cut out four squares, 7½in (19cm) in fabric.
- Cut out four squares, 6⅜in (16cm) in batting (wadding).
- Cut out a large and a small heart in different fabrics. You can use double-sided fusible interfacing for the appliqué but they will be less frayed than my appliqué.
- To make loops for hanging up the pot holders, cut off four belt straps from the denim jeans.
- Place a square of denim and a square of fabric, wrong sides together and draw up vertical, horizontal and both the diagonal lines.
- Fold aside the upper square, lay a piece of batting on to the centre of the lower square and replace the upper square.
- Pin together the three layers – denim, batting and fabric – and machine quilt along all the lines.
- On two of the blocks, fasten a large and a small appliqué heart (see template page 15) on the denim side using a straight seam, just within the edge of both hearts, through all three layers.

- Lay a block with heart appliqué together with a block without appliqué, wrong sides together.
- Now sew the blocks together around the edges with a ½in (1.25cm) seam allowance.
- Machine the four belt straps on in the uppermost corner, two on to each block. They may not be very practical for hanging up the pot holders but they add fun!
- Cut notches in the seam allowances, at distances of about ½in (1.25cm).
- Machine wash the pot holders at 40°C. Tumble drying is a good idea.

Denim Bag

In order to create colour variations this bag is made from two different pairs of denim as jeans often vary greatly with regard to colour.

Stitch as follows:
- Cut up the side or inner seams on the jeans, i.e., those seams that are not sewn double.
- Gently press the trouser legs and cut them off. One leg should be cut off at about 12in (30cm) and one at about 16in (40cm), along the leg's entire width.
- Cut out the fabric for the inside of the bag in corresponding sizes.
- Cut the batting (wadding) that goes between the layers of fabric to ½in (1.25cm) less than the fabrics, all the way round. This equals the seam allowance that you will cut up.
- Lay the inside fabric with the wrong side up, then the batting and finally the denim, with the wrong sides together.
- Quilt each part separately, either following pencilled lines or freehand. In addition, sew a seam around both pieces, ½in (1.25cm) from the edge, but not along the bottom edge.
- Sew both legs together to form a cylinder, by placing them on top of one another with about ½in (1.25cm) overlap and sew them together with a regular straight seam.

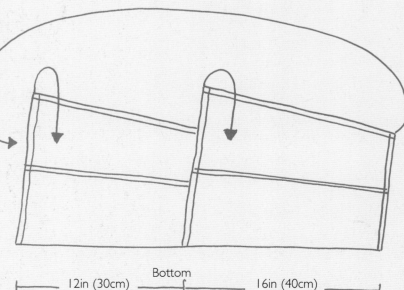

Bottom

|— 12in (30cm) —| |— 16in (40cm) —|
approx.   approx.

Bottom:

- Lay the bag out flat and measure its width. You need this measurement to find out the bottom's measurement. Multiply the width by two; this gives you the circumference. In order to find the right size for the bottom circle, you need to know the radius. To calculate the radius: circumference ÷ (2 × 3.14) = radius. Use the radius as a measurement and draw the circle on paper using a compass. This will be your pattern.
- Lay the pattern on the denim and inside fabric and cut out with a seam allowance of ½in (1.25cm) around the entire circle.
- Use the pattern (without seam allowance) to cut out the batting (wadding). If you want a stiffer bottom, you can iron on some extra fabric on either side of the batting with double-sided fusible interfacing.
- Lay the batting between the layers and quilt, for instance along diagonal lines.
- Sew the bottom on to the bag with seams facing outward, with ½in (1.25cm) seam allowance.

Handles:

- The handles are made of two waistbands, one from each pair of trousers.
- Cut off the waistbands at the seams and cut off the belt straps, keeping the buttons. The waistbands do not need to be identical in length, just sew them on to the bag so they end up being the same length.
- Fold down the extra 'ends' on the bag against the right side and sew on the handles.
- If the handles turn out too wide, you can fold them over double and sew a seam along the middle. The seam can start and end at the bag's edges.
- Cut notches in the seam allowances, at distances of about ½in (1.25cm).
- Machine wash the bag at 40°C. You can also tumble dry it.

The projects on these pages use the frayed-edge technique very effectively. The small bag sewn in denim and checked (chequered) fabric at the back of the photo (right) is the same size as the little bag on page 28, but this one has frayed edges.

Small Denim Bag

The little bag is perfect for all the small bits and pieces you need in your bag at any time and is just the right size for personal toiletries.

You will need:
Five 4in (10cm) squares of denim
Five 4in (10cm) squares of fabric for the inside
Five 2⅞in (7.3cm) squares of batting (wadding)
Two casings each 5 × 7in (13 × 17.5cm)
Two cords each about 14in (35cm) long

Stitch as follows:
- Follow the procedure for the frayed-edge technique for denim on page 13 and sew five blocks for the small bag.
- Sew the blocks together with one block for the bottom and four for the sides.
- Fold over the casings double on both sides until the width is 6in (15.5cm).
- Press them double, wrong sides together and sew a seam ½in (1.25cm) from the fold.

- Sew the casing on with a ½in (1.25cm) seam allowance facing the right side.
- Cut notches in the seam allowances at distances of about ½in (1.25cm).
- Machine wash the bag at 40°C. You can also tumble dry it.
- Thread in a cord from both sides all the way round and tie them together.

Spectacle/Mobile Phone Case

Sew this case together in the same way and with the same measurements as the small denim bag but using only four blocks. Two of the blocks must be quilted ½in (1.25cm) along one edge, which will become the opening for the case.

Sew two and two blocks together. Place them wrong sides together and sew them together: side–bottom–side. Make sure that the right blocks are next to the opening. Cut up the seam allowance and machine wash at 40°C.

Tiny Denim Bag

You will need:
Two pieces of denim 6 × 10in (15.5 × 5.5cm)
Two pieces of checked fabric 6 × 10in (5 × 25.5cm)
Four pieces of fabric for bag inside, 6 × 10in (15.5 × 25.5cm)
Batting (wadding), preferably cotton, four pieces 4⅞ × 10in (12.4 × 25.5cm)
Fabric for the casings, two casings 5 × 11in (13 × 28cm) Cord, two 25in (64cm) lengths

Stitch as follows:

- Sew four blocks in the frayed-edge technique, two blocks with denim/inside fabric and two blocks checked/inside fabric. See page 13 for instructions on frayed-edge technique in denim. Only fray the long edges, not the top or the bottom, where the batting (wadding) should go all the way to the edge.
- Sew together the four blocks, with alternating denim and checked fabrics, to form a cylinder.
- Sew the tiny bag's bottom piece by folding in pleats from all the sides so they meet in the middle (see the diagram on page 27). Sew the seam and then zigzag

stitch across the seam allowance.
- Double hem the casings on both sides, until the width is 10in (25.5cm).
- Press them double, wrong sides together and sew a seam 1in (2.5cm) from the fold.
- Sew on the casings from the bag's inside.
- Fold the casings over to the outsides and hem in the seam.
- Machine stitch the casing to the very edge and sew an extra seam along the edge of the little bag itself. This will cover the raw edges inside the hem.
- Thread in a cord from both sides and tie together.

17

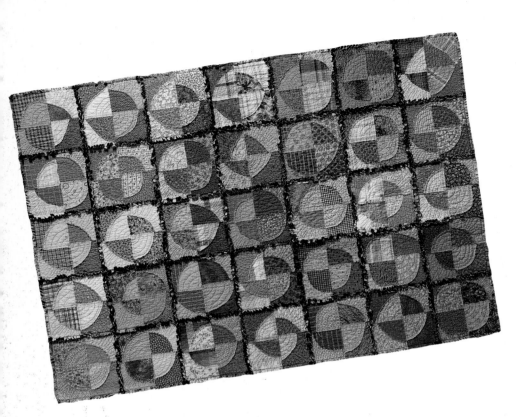

Round Frayed-Edge Throw

47 x 65in (120 x 165cm) approx.

This throw is both rough and soft at the same time. It looks rough because the seam allowance has been cut up and frayed in the wash. It is soft because of the underlying structure in the quilting and the pink, beige, green and light turquoise colours.

Stitch as follows:

- Cut out 140 squares, 6in (15.25cm): seventy light and seventy dark fabrics.
- Pair up the fabrics, one light and one dark square and lay them on top of one another, right side to wrong side.
- With the right side facing up, freehand cut a quarter circle through both squares – i.e., not a perfectly round shape.
- Arrange the pieces into two square blocks and swap around the quarter circles, so they are next to different fabrics.
- Place the quarter circles just over the other part of the block, with an overlap of about ½in (1.25cm), right side to wrong side.
- Machine stitch the quarter circle with a seam allowance of about ¼in (0.7cm) from the raw edge.
- Cut off any superfluous fabric so that the blocks have straight lines.
- Pair up two new fabrics and sew them together in the same way.
- Arrange all four blocks together into a new and larger block and sew them together with an overlap of about ½in (1.25cm), right side to wrong side.
- Do the same with all of the remaining squares.
- Now cut all the blocks to the same size. I cut mine to 10½in (26.5cm) square because that suited my blocks.
- Quilt each block separately with batting (wadding) and backing. Cut the backing to the size of the block itself, 10½ x 10½in (26.5 x 26.5cm) and cut the batting 1⅛in (2.8cm) smaller – i.e. 35 squares of batting 9⅜in (23.8cm).
- Place the batting in the centre between the block and the back piece and freehand quilt on your sewing machine.
- Place the blocks, back to back and sew them together with a seam allowance of ½in (1.25cm).
- Sew two rounds of straight seam around the entire throw, ½in (1.25cm) from the edge.
- Cut notches into the seam allowances, at distances of about ½in (1.25cm).
- Machine wash the throw at 40°C. You can also tumble dry it to enhance the frayed-edge effect.

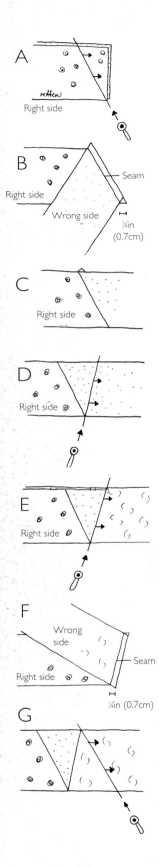

A
rettfen
Right side

B
Right side
Wrong side
Seam
¼in (0.7cm)

C
Right side

D
Right side

E
Right side

F
Wrong side
Right side
Seam
¼in (0.7cm)

G

Rows of Jags

Sewing rows of jags is fun. The striking patterns are created by laying and cutting fabric strips, as described here.

Stitch a row of jags as follows:

- Using ¼in (0.7cm) seam allowances cut out the strips – the width varies from project to project. The strips are 3½in (9cm) wide on the blue and red runners on page 23 and 24 and for the blue house wall hanging (right). The strips on the bag and cushion on page 26 are 5½in (4cm) wide. The strips don't need to be all that long if you have many types of fabrics. You will need both light and dark strips. Follow Figs A–G.
- A – lay a light and a dark strip next to one another, right side to wrong side. Cut a slanting line through both strips. This line will be one of the jag's sides.
- B – lay one of the strips on to the other, right side to right side, in the slanting incision you made. Shift them a little so they cross exactly ¼in (0.7cm) from the edge.
- C – gently press the seam and seam allowance one way. You now have a complete strip with a light and a dark part.
- D – for the time being, don't cut the light strip but a slanting cut into the dark strip, giving a triangle. The incision doesn't need to be at the same angle as the previous one but it must start in the previous seam, so it forms a jag, not a truncated jag.
- E – lay a new light strip under the dark/light one, right side to wrong side, exactly on top of one another. Cut into the new, light strip, like the dark one's angle.
- F – lay them together, right side to right side in the incision just made; shift them ¼in (0.7cm) and sew them together.
- G – press the seams one way and continue with alternating light and dark strips, until your row of jags is long enough for the house wall hanging, or you have enough for a runner, bag or cushion.

Blue House Wall Hanging

15½ x 19½in (39.5 x 49.5cm)

Tidy up your fabric shelves or dig in your remnant basket – there is bound to be something you can use for this wall hanging.

Stitch as follows:

- Refer to the diagrams overleaf before cutting out your fabrics.
  A – window: 3½ x 3½in (9 x 9cm). Cut in two, freehand.
  B – between and on either side of the windows – 3½ x 4½in (9 x 11.5cm). Cut in three, freehand.
  C – house wall: 6 x 6in (15 x 15cm). Cut off a third freehand. Make the top of the wall by cutting two triangles off the remaining piece.
  D – roof ridge: 7½ x 2in (19 x 5cm). Cut this in two lengthwise, freehand.
  E – background: 3½ x 6in (9 x 15cm). Cut this in two lengthwise, freehand.
  F – background: 6 x 6in (15 x 15cm). Cut along the diagonal line, using a ruler.
- Sew the pieces together to a house block. Cut all the seams to size after pressing them, giving a straight line to follow when sewing. Cut the house block to size, to 8 x 9in (20.25 x 22.75cm).
- For the rest of the wall hanging, cut out according to the measurements on the large diagram and sew the pieces together.
- Cut out 3½in (9cm) strips for the jagged edge. I sewed on the appliqué sun with visible raw edges; use a straight seam for sewing these on. I used double-sided fusible interfacing when making the sun appliqué (see page 10 for technique).
- Machine quilt the hanging closely freehand and finish it off with a binding.

Lise Design
3282 KVELDE
TLF. 33112438

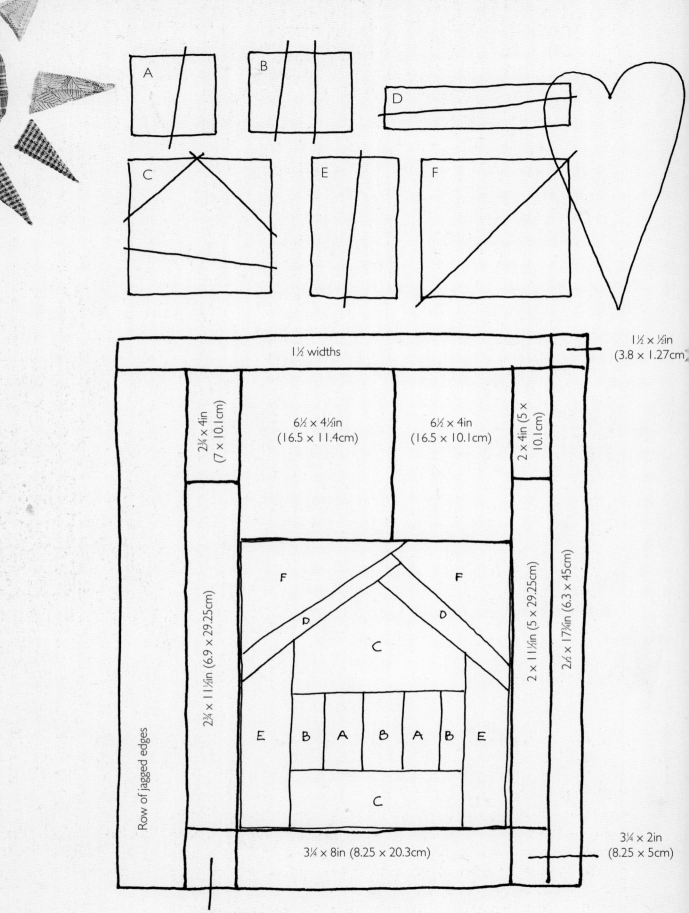

A

B

D

C

E

F

1½ × ½in
(3.8 × 1.27cm)

1½ widths

2¾ × 4in
(7 × 10.1cm)

6½ × 4½in
(16.5 × 11.4cm)

6½ × 4in
(16.5 × 10.1cm)

2 × 4in (5 ×
10.1cm)

2¾ × 11½in (6.9 × 29.25cm)

Row of jagged edges

F

F

D

D

C

E B A B A B E

C

2 × 11½in (5 × 29.25cm)

2½ × 17¾in (6.3 × 45cm)

3¼ × 8in (8.25 × 20.3cm)

3¼ × 2in
(8.25 × 5cm)

3¼ × 2¾in (8.25 × 7cm)

Blue Runner with Jags

15 x 34in (38 x 86.5cm)

Once you have started working with jags you will find them addictive, so you might as well sew a runner or two...

Stitch as follows:

- Cut the strips for the row of jags, 3½in (9cm) wide, using both dark and light blue fabrics.
- Sew eight rows of jags, following the procedure described on page 20. The rows should be as long as the desired width of the runner – mine are 15in (38cm).
- Cut out seven strips, 2in (5cm) wide and with the length equivalent to the runner's width.
- Sew the rows of jags together, with strips in between.
- Machine quilt the runner freehand, using multicoloured thread if you want.
- Finish the runner with a binding.

Red Runner with Jags

13 × 45½in (33 × 115.5cm)

This gorgeous runner has a central panel of seven square blocks in colours including yellow, orange and red combined with olive green. The colours for the rows of jags range from pink/cerise to red and light fabrics in pale purple and turquoise/green. The picture also shows an attractive cushion made using the same techniques.

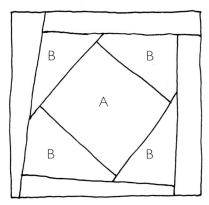

Stitch as follows:

- First of all, judge by eye a square measuring 4 × 4in (10 × 10cm). Cut out three squares on this judgement. One will be A, the other two will become B once you have cut them along diagonal lines.
- Sew all four B triangles on to A (see diagram above).
- Cut the blocks to give you straight lines; they will probably be slightly askew, which is quite all right.
- Sew on strips that are more or less 1½in (4cm) wide.
- Cut the blocks to 7 × 7in (17.75 × 17.75cm), making sure all corners are at right angles.
- Make the rows of jags as for the blue runner on page 23, apart from the length, which for this red runner must be of the same length as the seven square blocks.
- Machine quilt the runner with crossing straight seams going from one long side to the other.
- Finish off with a bright binding to match your fabrics.

25

Cushion with Jags

If you have an extra house block from page 20, sew a few extra rounds of strips around the house and you can make a cushion in no time at all.

Stitch as follows:
- Cut out strips 5½in (14cm) wide for rows of jagged edges, using light and dark fabrics.
- Sew three rows of jags, following the procedure described on page 20. The rows should be about 15½in (40cm) long.
- Sew together three rows of jagged edges to a cushion, making it as square as possible.
- Machine quilt the cushion freehand.
- Make a back piece for the cushion, closing it either with a zip or buttons.
- Sew the cushion together with a binding by laying the pieces wrong sides together; machine sew on the binding from the cushion's front side; fold it over double to the back and sew it on by hand.

Little Bag with Jags

Stitch as follows:
- Cut out strips 5½in (14cm) wide for jagged edges, using light and dark fabrics (mine were from Bali).
- Sew two rows of jagged edges, following the instructions on page 20. The jagged edges should be about 10in (25.5cm) long.
- Cut out two rectangles in a dark fabric, with the same measurements as the jagged edges, 5½ × 10in (14 × 25.5cm).
- Sew together alternating rows of jags and fabric pieces to a single piece.
- Quilt the piece with batting (wadding) and backing freehand with a multicoloured thread.
- Cut the entire piece to size.
- Sew the piece together to form a cylinder with a seam allowance of about ¼in (0.7cm). You can zigzag across the seam allowance with your machine.
- Sew the bottom of the bag by folding in pleats on either side so they meet in the middle (see diagram below). Sew the seam. Zigzag across the seam allowance with your machine.
- Make the casing out of two rectangles, 5 × 11in (13 × 28cm). Hem in double on both sides until the width is 10in (25.5cm), i.e., ¼in (0.7cm) twice.
- Iron the casings double, wrong sides together and sew a 1in seam (2.5cm) from the folding edge.
- Sew the casings on from the inside of the bag then fold the casing over to outside and hem in the seam.
- Machine stitch the casings down along the very edge and sew an extra seam along the edge of the little bag itself. This will cover the raw edges.
- Thread in a cord from both sides, all the way round and tie them together. Each cord is about 25in (64cm) long.

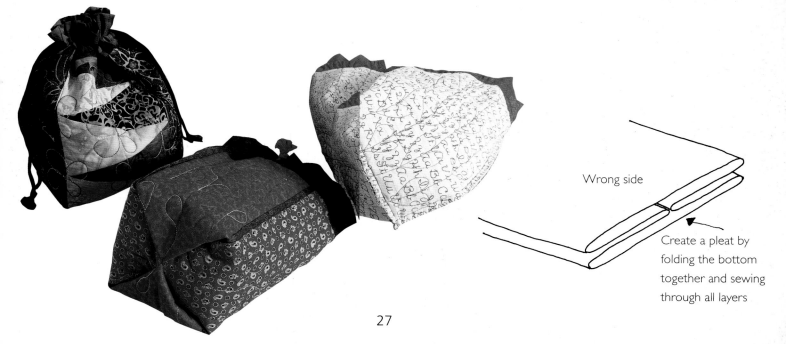

Wrong side

Create a pleat by folding the bottom together and sewing through all layers

27

Large and Small Bags

You can make the little bag described on the previous page without jags, or make a smaller one. On the following three pages are five different bags. They are all sewn together the same way but have different measurements.

Red/black and Red/blue Bag

You will need:
Two fabrics for the bag, two pieces of each fabric
5½ × 10in (14 × 25.5cm)
One fabric for the casing, two casings 5 × 11in
(13 × 28cm)
One fabric for the inside of the little bag, about
12 × 22in (30 × 56cm)
One fabric for the edging, four strips 1 × 10in
(2.5 × 25.5cm)
Batting (wadding), preferably cotton, about 12 × 22in
(30 × 56cm)
Cord, two 25in (64cm) lengths

Stitch as follows:
- Press the edging double, wrong sides together. Sew the four pieces of fabric together; they should be placed alternately, with the edging in between, to create a single piece.
- Quilt the piece with batting (wadding) and backing freehand with multicoloured thread.
- Cut the piece to size.
- Sew the piece together into a cylinder with a seam allowance of ¼in (0.7cm). You can zigzag across the seam allowance.
- Sew the bottom of the bag by folding in pleats from both sides so they meet in the middle (see diagram page 27). Sew the seam. Zigzag across the seam allowance.
- Make a double hem in the casings on both sides, until the width is 10in (25.5cm), i.e., ¼in (0.7cm) twice.
- Press the doubled, wrong sides together, and sew a seam 1in (2.5cm) from the folding edge.
- Sew on the casings from the inside of the bag.
- Fold the casings over to the outside and hem in the seams.
- Stitch the casings down with the sewing machine at the very edge and sew an additional seam along the edge of the bag itself, to cover the raw edges.
- Thread in a cord from both sides, all the way round and tie them together.

Small Flower Bag

The largest of the little bags with small flowers has the same measurements as the pink checked one on page 31, but the smallest has the following measurements.

You will need:
One piece of fabric for the bag, 4 x 8½in (10 x 21.5cm)
One piece of fabric for the casing, two casings of 3½ x 5in (9 x 13cm)
One piece of fabric for the inside of the bag, about 5½ x 10in (14 x 25.5cm)
Batting (wadding), preferably cotton, about 5½ x 10in (14 x 25.5cm)
Cord, two 11in (28cm) lengths of silk ribbon

Stitch as follows:
■ Place the fabric for the outside together with batting (wadding) and fabric for the inside and machine quilt the piece.
■ Follow the procedure for the red/black and red/blue bag, but make a double hem in the casing on both sides, so the width is 4in (10cm), i.e.,¼in (0.7cm) twice.
■ Thread in a cord from both sides, all the way round and tie them together.

Cerise and Purple Bag

You will need:
One piece of fabric for the bag, 8 × 16½in (20.5 × 42cm)
One piece of fabric for the casing, two casings of
4½ × 9in (11.5 × 23cm)
One piece of fabric for the inside of the bag, about
9½ × 18in (24 × 46cm)
Batting (wadding), preferably cotton, about 9½ × 18in
(24 × 46cm)
Cord or ribbon, two 19in (48cm) lengths

Stitch as follows:
■ Place the fabric for the outside together with batting
(wadding) and fabric for the inside and machine quilt
the piece.
■ Follow the procedure for the red/black and red/blue
bag on page 28, but make a double hem in the casing
on both sides, so the width is 8in (20.5cm), i.e. ¼in
(0.7cm) twice.
■ Thread in a cord from both sides, all the way round
and tie them together.

Green Bag with Flowers

You will need:
One piece of fabric for the bag, 6 × 12½in (15.5 × 32cm)
One piece of fabric for the casing, two casings of
4½ × 7in (11.5 × 18cm)
One piece of fabric for the inside of the bag, about
7½ × 14in (19 × 35.5cm)
Batting (wadding), preferably cotton, about 7½ × 14in
(19 × 35.5cm)
Cord, two 18in (46cm) lengths of silk ribbon

Stitch as follows:
■ Place the fabric for the outside together with batting
(wadding) and the fabric for the inside and machine
quilt the piece.
■ Follow the procedure for red/black and red/blue bag
on page 28, but make a double hem in the casing on
both sides, so the width is 6in (15.5cm), i.e. ¼in
(0.7cm) twice.
■ Thread in ribbon from both sides, all the way round
and tie them together.

Pink Check Bag

You will need:
One piece of fabric for the bag, 5 × 10½in (13 × 27cm)
One piece of fabric for the casing, two casings of 4 × 6in
(10 × 15.5cm)
One piece of fabric for the inside of the bag, about
6½ × 12in (16.5 × 30.5cm)
Batting (wadding), preferably cotton, about 6½ × 12in
(16.5 × 30.5cm)
Cord, two 13in (33cm) lengths

Stitch as follows:
■ Place the fabric for the outside together with batting
(wadding) and the fabric for the inside and machine
quilt the piece.
■ Follow the procedure for the red/black and red/blue
bag on page 28, but make a double hem in the
casing on both sides, so the width is 5in (13.75cm),
i.e. ¼in (0.7cm) twice.
■ Thread in a cord from both sides, all the way round
and tie them together.

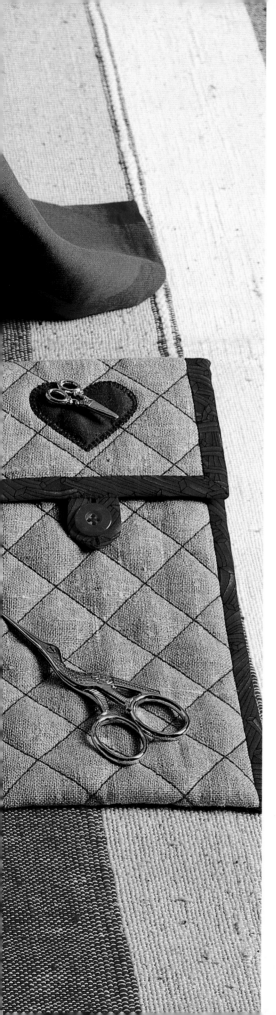

Linen Sewing Set

This set consists of a sewing kit, a little bag, a case for needles and thread and a scissors case. Everything is sewn in linen and decorated with appliqué hearts (see page 10 for using fusible interfacing). If you want a different version of this kit, look at page 40 for ideas — there's an example there made in fabric from the 1930s. On page 36 you will find the sewing case in denim.

Sewing Kit

Stitch as follows:

- Cut out one 9 x 13in (23 x 33cm) piece in linen, batting (wadding) and inside fabric.
- Quilt the piece with parallel diagonal lines in both directions, with intervals of 1¼in (3.25cm). Cut the piece to size to 8 x 12in (20 x 30.5cm).
- Cut out four appliqué hearts using the template on page 35, and sew them on to the bag using double-sided fusible interfacing and an appliqué seam. Place three of the hearts on one side and one on the other.
- Cut two strips, 1½ x 8in (4 x 20cm) and sew on a strip along each of the short sides. First, sew on the strips from the wrong side (the inside), then fold the strips over to the outside and hem in the seam.
- Machine sew on a 10in (25cm) long zip along the short side. Make sure that the same length of the zip sticks out on either side. Seal each end with a double silk ribbon or similar.
- Make a pleat at the bottom (see diagram below) and sew the side seams. Zigzag across the side seams to finish.

Inside

1in (2.5cm)

Making a pleat on the bottom of the sewing kit

Little Linen Bag

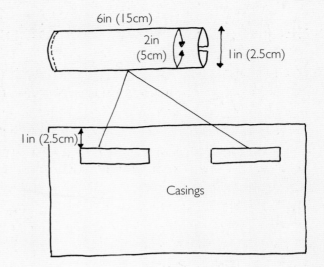

Casings

Stitch as follows:

- Cut out one 9 × 17½in (23 × 45cm) piece in linen, batting (wadding) and inside fabric.
- Quilt the piece with parallel diagonal lines in both directions, with intervals of 1¼in (3.25cm). Multicoloured thread looks good on linen.
- Cut the piece to 8 × 16½in (20 × 42cm).
- Cut out six appliqué hearts (template opposite) and sew them on to the bag using double-sided fusible interfacing and an appliqué seam. You can place three hearts on either side of the bag.
- Cut out fabric for two casings, two pieces of 2 × 6in (5 × 15.25cm). Fold in a 1in (2.5cm) hem on both short sides and machine stitch them down. Fold and press both casings to a width of 1in (2.5cm). Machine stitch them on to the bag with stitches at the very outside of the folded edge (see diagram).
- Sew the piece together into a cylinder. Zigzag across the seam allowance or sew a strip into the seam: cut the strip to a width of 1¾in (4.5cm), sew it into the seam, fold it over the raw edges and fasten it by hand with small stitches.
- Make a circular pattern for the bottom with radius of

2⅞in (7.25cm) with seam allowance. The bottom is made of linen, batting (wadding) and fabric for the inside. Make the bottom a little larger than the pattern and quilt it in both directions diagonally. Cut it out in accordance with the pattern.
- Now sew the bottom to the bag with wrong sides together (insides together) and cover the seam with a binding 1½in (4cm) wide.
- Sew a binding along the edge, using a strip 1½ × 16in (4 × 42cm).
- Thread in two cords, 22in (55cm) long.

Needle Case

Stitch as follows:
- Cut out a piece of linen, batting (wadding) and inside fabric, all about 6 x 13in (15 x 33cm).
- Quilt the piece with parallel diagonal lines in both directions, at intervals of about 1¼in (3.25cm).
- Cut the piece to size, to 5¼ x 12in (13.5 x 30.5cm).
- Cut a strip 1½ x 5¾in (4 x 14.5cm); enough to cover one of the raw edges.
- Sew on the strip on one of the short sides, as a binding, so it covers the raw edge.
- Cut out an appliqué heart and sew it on using double-sided fusible interfacing (see page 10) and a decorative stitch.
- Fold up the side with the folding edge 4in (10cm).
- Sew a 1½in (4cm) wide binding around the three remaining sides. If you want to include a loop for closing the case, sew this on now. Make the loop from a strip 1½ x 3in (4 x 7.5cm), folded double, twice, so the width is about ⅜in (1cm).
- Sew on a button to match the loop.
- Make the pincushion underneath the flap out of two fabrics and some batting (wadding), tacked (basted) around with small stitches by hand. Sew the pincushion to the cover with small stitches at four points, securing the thread with a knot.

Scissors Case

Stitch as follows:
- Cut out a piece of linen, batting (wadding) and inside fabric, all about 5 x 22in (13 x 56cm).
- Quilt the piece with parallel, diagonal lines in both directions, with intervals of about 1¼in (3.25cm).
- Cut the piece to size, 4½ x 21in (11.5 x 53.5cm).
- Now follow the instructions the sewing kit, except up the side with the binding 9in (23cm).

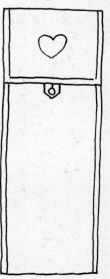

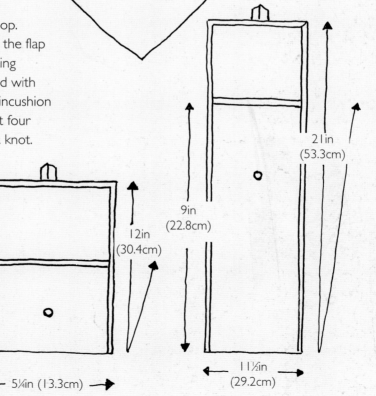

Pincushion

Heart for appliqué

21in (53.3cm)

12in (30.4cm)

9in (22.8cm)

4in (10.1cm)

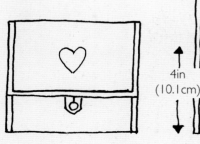

5¼in (13.3cm)

11½in (29.2cm)

Denim Gifts

Small make-up bags are excellent gifts for young girls and the sewing kit is perfect for a clever seamstress! If you prefer the models in attractive 1930s fabric, turn to page 40.

Denim Sewing Kit

You will need:
One piece of denim, 5¾ × 12in
(14.5 × 30.5cm)
One piece of fabric for the inside, 5¾ × 12in
(14.5 × 30.5cm)
One piece of batting (wadding), preferably
cotton, 4¾ × 11½in (12 × 29cm)
Three belt straps from a pair of jeans
One small coin pocket from a pair of jeans
One small nice-looking label from an item of
clothing
One cotton strip, 1½ × 5¾in (4 × 14.5cm),
to cover one of the raw edges
Some extra batting (wadding) for under the
label, so it becomes a pincushion

Stitch as follows:
- Follow the procedure for frayed-edge
  technique for denim on page 13 and quilt
  the case with several zigzag seams going
  lengthwise. On one of the short sides, the
  batting (wadding) should reach right to the
  very edge.
- Sew the strip on to the short side with the
  batting reaching the very edge, as a binding.
- Fold up the side with the binding 4in
  (10cm).
- Find a place for the coin pocket – it should
  be inside the kit. Machine sew it on.
- While the kit is folded, you will also find the
  position for the belt straps that will be the
  closing mechanism. Position two of them
  next to each other and sew them together

with two seams at one end and sew on a button also at this end. Sew on the other end to the lid of the kit with two seams. Place the last belt strap across the case at the very bottom of the case, so the belt straps you have sewn together can be tucked underneath. The button will hold the strap in place.

- Lay some batting (wadding) underneath the label and sew it in place underneath the lid.
- Sew together the kit, using a seam allowance of ½in (1.25cm).
- Cut notches in the seam allowance at intervals of about ½in (1.25cm).
- Machine wash the kit at 40°C and then tumble dry it.

Denim Make-Up Case

You will need:
Some denim
Fabric for the inside
Bias binding or fabric for bias binding
Some cotton batting (wadding)
A label or two
Two belt straps
One pocket from the denim trousers
One zip, about 8in (20cm) long
Denim needles for your sewing machine

Stitch as follows:
- Cut out two pieces each of denim and inside fabric, each 5½ × 6¾in (14 × 17.25cm) height × width.
- Cut out two pieces of batting (wadding), 4⅞ × 5⅝in (12.5 × 14.25cm).
- Out of denim, batting and lining fabric, sew two blocks in frayed-edge technique (see page 13). The piece of batting should be right next to the denim and inside fabric on one of the sides and equidistant from the edge on the three other sides. The opening will be where the batting reaches the edge. These blocks will make up the case itself.
- Cut out denim and inside fabric, one piece of each, 5¼ × 2½in (13.5 × 6.5cm).

- Cut out one piece of batting, 4⅛ × 1⅜in (10.5 × 3.5cm).
- Using the frayed-edge technique, sew a block out of denim, inside fabric and batting. The piece of batting should lie in the centre – this will be the bottom of the make-up case.
- Copy the pattern for the make-up case from page 144. Lay the pattern on the two blocks for the case itself, with the curved line where the batting reaches the edge. Cut it along the curved line – this is the case's opening.
- Sew on a bias binding on the two curved parts. Do this by cutting out a strip on the bias from the fabric, width 1½in (4cm) and iron it double, wrong sides together. Sew the strip on to the case from the inside, with the raw edges towards the opening of the case. Fold the strip over to the outside and sew it on with a machine stitch.
- It is easiest to sew the zip on by hand with small stitches from the wrong side, sewing down the edge of the zip.
- If you want to decorate the case with small pockets or labels, do this now.
- Sew the case together, using a ½in (1.25cm) seam allowance throughout. First, sew the bottom to the side blocks, then the side seams and finally the corner seams. To make it easier to sew the corner seams, cut notches into the side blocks. Don't forget – seam allowance on the outside.
- Cut off the zip if it is too long and sew on a belt strap on both sides of the case so that the end of the zip is covered.
- Cut notches in the seam allowance and machine wash the case at 40°C.

Denim Sponge Bags

For both bags you will need:
Some denim
Fabric for the inside
Bias binding or fabric to make bias binding
Some cotton batting (wadding)
One or two labels
Two belt straps
One pocket from the jeans
One zip, about 10–12in (25–30cm) for a little bag and about 12in (30cm) for a large bag
Denim needles for your sewing machine

Stitch as follows for the small bag:
- Cut out two pieces each of denim and inside fabric, each 8¼ × 9¼in (21 × 23.5cm) height × width.
- Cut out two pieces of batting (wadding), 7⅝ × 8⅛in (19.5 × 20.75cm).
- Out of denim, batting and inside fabric, sew two blocks in the frayed-edge technique (see page 13). The piece of batting should reach the edge on one of the sides and be at the same distance from the edge on the other three sides. The opening will be where the batting reaches the edge. These blocks make up the case itself.

- Cut out denim and inside fabric, one piece of each 6¾ × 3½in (17.25 × 9cm).
- Cut out one piece of batting, 5⅝ × 2⅞in (14.25 × 7.25cm).
- Using the frayed-edge technique, sew a block out of denim, inside fabric and batting. The piece of batting should lie in the centre – this will be the bottom of the bag.
- Copy the pattern for the small sponge bag from page 144.
- Lay the pattern on the two blocks for the case itself, with the curved line where the batting reaches the edge. Cut it along the curved line – this is the case's opening.
- Sew on a bias binding on both openings. Do this by cutting out a strip on the bias from the fabric, width 1½in (4cm) and ironing it double, wrong side together. Sew the strip on to the case from the inside, with the raw edges towards the opening of the case. Fold the strip over to the outside and machine stitch it on.
- It is easiest to hand sew on the zip, from the wrong side with small stitches, sewing down the zip edge.
- If you want to decorate the case with small pockets or labels, do this now.
- Sew the case together using a ½in (1.25cm) seam allowance throughout. First, sew the bottom to the

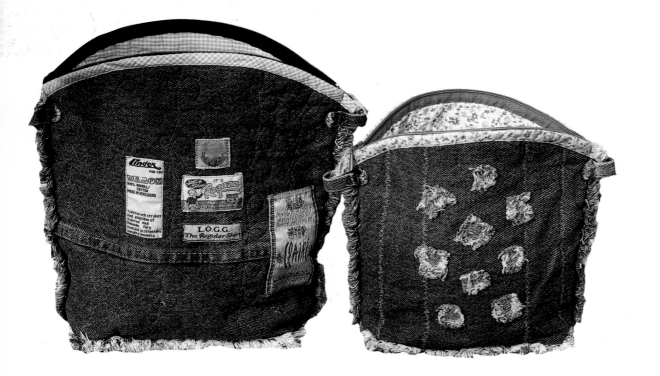

side blocks, then the side seams and finally the corner seams. To make it easier to sew the corner seams, cut notches into the side blocks. Don't forget that the seam allowance should be on the outside.

- Cut off the zip if it is too long and sew on a belt strap on both sides of the case so that the end of the zip is covered.
- Cut notches in the seam allowances and machine wash the bag at 40°C.

Stitch as follows for the large bag:

- Cut out two pieces each of denim and inside fabric, each 10½ x 11in (26.75 x 28cm) height x width.
- Cut out two pieces of batting (wadding), 9⅞ x 9⅞in (25 x 25cm).

- Out of denim, batting and lining fabric, sew two blocks in frayed-edge technique (see page 13). The piece of batting should reach the edge on one of the sides and be at the same distance from the three other edges. The opening will be where the batting reaches the edge. These blocks make up the bag itself.
- Cut out denim and inside fabric, one piece of each, 7½ x 4½in (19 x 11.5cm) and one piece of batting, 6⅜ x 3⅜in (16.25 x 8.5cm).
- Continue to follow the procedure for the small sponge bag, but use the large sponge bag pattern on page 144.

Ellen's Gifts

In order to show you more versions of the sewing kit, little bag, make-up bag and sponge bags, some fine models were sewn by Ellen Borge, a dear friend of many years' standing who shares my passion for patchwork. It is a boon having somebody who can help with advice and making models. I hope Ellen's work inspires you. The projects are all made of 1¼in (3.25cm) squares. She has also changed some of the models a little with regard to size, but you will find the basic patterns for the sponge bags and make-up cases on page 144 and instructions for the little bag and sewing case on pages 34 and 35.

1930s Bedspread

45 × 84in (114.5 × 213.5cm)

A while I go, I was given a nice little pile of small pieces of fabric. The fabrics were all inspired by the 1930s and I wanted to try and use them all in a single bedspread. After some thinking, I decided to cut all the pieces into three. The bedspread has a lovely, soft backing of brushed cotton and is perfect for a blanket on cold evenings.

My pieces for this bedspread measured 8 × 6in (20.5 × 15cm) and I had a total of forty-five pieces. I cut up the pieces in exactly the same manner – 2in (5cm), 2½in (6.5cm) and 3½in (9cm). I mixed and distributed the pieces into four columns, all the same length. Two of my columns ended up ½in (1.25cm) too long so I simply cut them to the size of the other two lengths. Between each column of small pieces I sewed on a column of the same fabric, width 4½in (11.5cm). If you do not have a fabric that is the right length, simply join them together until you have the right measurement.

To make the bedspread large enough for a single bed, I sewed on a 6in (15cm) border around the entire bedspread, first a border on each of the long sides and then on the short sides. I did this with the same fabric as the one for the columns between the small patches. The bedspread has yellow backing in brushed cotton and the batting (wadding) is made of cotton.

Once the bedspread was pieced, I sent it to a company specializing in quilting and had it returned ready quilted. (Look on the web or in patchwork magazines for such companies in your area.) When the bedspread returned I sewed on the bindings myself and made them of striped fabric that had some of the colours of the rest of the bedspread. I think it looks smart and is nice and soft – as well as being a souvenir of the present I was given.

Open Bag in Denim

Stitch as follows:

- Cut out eighteen 6in (15.25cm) squares of fabric. Colours that contrast with the denim colour are good.
- Sew them together into a single piece, consisting of three horizontal rows with six squares each.
- Machine quilt the piece along the seams with batting (wadding) and fabric for the back piece/inside.
- Cut out eighteen 8½in (21.5cm) squares in denim.
- Sew each square to an X block. To do this, fold the square double, wrong sides together and sew together the short side with a seam allowance of ½in (1.25cm). You now have a piece that looks like an oblong pocket. Open up the pocket, pull the short sides together and sew the seam, with a ½in (1.25cm) seam allowance. The block is square again and now has an X from corner to corner, with the seam allowance outside. Its measurements are about 5¼in (13.25cm) square. Gently press the block.
- On the piece you quilted, lay an X block on each square.
- Machine sew on all the X blocks along all four sides.
- Sew together the bag by folding the piece together, right side to right side, with nine blocks on either side of the bag and sew the side seams. Include a 1¾in (4.5cm) wide strip when sewing the side seam. Fold this over the seam's raw edges and sew it by hand.
- Sew a binding around the bag's opening.

Handles:

- To make the handles, start by sewing some fabric tapes. Cut out eight strips of 2 × 6in (5 × 15.25cm), iron them double, wrong sides together and iron the seam allowance in towards the centre on both the long sides and sew a seam at the very edge.
- Cut out two 8in (20cm) lengths of the waistband on the denim.
- Place two tapes in each end of the waistbands and sew them on by machine.
- Fasten the handles to the bag on the outside by placing them under a belt strap from the jeans and sewing two seams along the straps.
- Cut notches into the seam allowances on the X blocks at a distance of ½in (1.25cm).
- Machine wash the bag at 40°C and give it a few gentle rounds in the tumble drier.

A Peaceful Christmas Holiday

16½ x 21½in (42 x 54.5cm)

This delightful wall hanging would be perfect in the festive season, bringing a welcoming glow to any house. On a similar theme, why not stitch an apron, runner and place mats (see overleaf).

Stitch as follows:

■ A – cut out 3½ x 16in (9 x 40.5cm) of red checked fabric.

■ B – cut out nine rectangles, 4½ x 6½in (11.5 x 16.5cm), six in white fabrics and three in red.

■ C – cut out six rectangles, 2¼ x 6½in (5.75 x 16.5cm) in red fabric.

■ Sew the hanging together in accordance with the diagram, top right.

■ With your sewing machine, write 'A peaceful Christmas holiday' freehand in any language you desire and also draw a 'frame' in which to position the design. Use an embroidery/free-motion quilting foot.

■ Secure the appliqué design using double-sided fusible interfacing (see page 10). Then sew on the design with a machine seam or by hand.

■ Machine quilt the hanging. You can quilt the frame with gently curved lines and you can machine quilt freehand on the white background area around the designs.

■ Finish off with a binding.

Christmas Apron

This Christmas apron is sewed in 100% linen and decorated with hearts and buttons and designs from page 45. There is also an appliqué of a snowman, hoping that Christmas will last until Easter. The apron is edged with bias binding – you will need about 5½yd (5m) in total.

Draw up the pattern full size, basing it on the diagram on page 145. The pockets, including seam allowances, are 7 × 8in (18 × 20cm). Fold the pocket in to 6¼ × 6¼in (16 × 16cm), with a large hem at the top. Each of the straps is 2½ × 23in (6.5 × 60cm). Press them double, wrong side to wrong side and edge with bias binding. The neck band is the same width as the waist straps, but adjust as necessary. Mine is 28in (70cm).

Star Runner in Linen
14 × 30in (36 × 76cm)

Stitch as follows:

- Cut out a piece of linen 14 × 30in (36 × 76cm).
- Decorate with machine stitching and sew several straight seams from one short side to the other. Black thread works well for this.
- Cut out twelve 4in (10cm) squares in red fabric for the border.
- Sew the squares together into two rows, one with eight squares and another with four squares. Divide each row in two lengthwise, with a width of 2in (5cm). You now have two short and two long strips.
- Draw a pencilled line around the entire runner, 1½in (3.75cm) from the edge.
- Lay the two longest strips along the pencilled line, right side to right side on the linen.

46

- Sew down the strips with a seam allowance of ¼in (0.7cm). Press the strips over the linen with the right side up.
- Do the same with the two short strips; they will cover the end of the long strips.
- Trace over nine or ten stars from page 145 on to double-sided fusible interfacing and iron them on to purple or red fabrics. Machine sew the appliqué stars on, with a close zigzag seam.
- You can machine quilt the runner but use a neutral-coloured thread that matches the linen colour, so the quilting seam doesn't stand out too much.
- Finish off with a bright binding.

Star Place Mat in Linen

Stitch as follows:
- Cut out a piece of linen, 12 × 16in (30 × 40cm) and two strips, 1½ × 12in (4 × 30cm).
- Place the strips along the short sides of the mat. Sew them on with silk ribbon, by sewing a seam on the very edges of the silk ribbon.
- Decorate with straight seams and appliqué stars, as for the runner.
- Machine quilt the place mat, with a discreetly coloured thread.
- Finish off with a binding.

Runner in Lively Colours
14 x 45½in (35.5 x 115.5cm)

Stitch as follows:
- Cut out fifteen fabric pieces, 3½ x 11in (28 x 9cm), in reddish-orange, red and dark pink.
- Cut out fifteen squares, 3½in (9cm), in purple fabrics.
- Sew the rectangles together with the squares, to finish up with fifteen oblong blocks.
- You can sew the runner together in the regular way, block to block, or you can sew the blocks together and quilt the runner at the same time. If you sew the blocks together and quilt them at the same time, you need a piece of fabric (the back side of the runner) and a piece of batting (wadding) that is a little larger in size than the completed runner, 16 x 47in (41 x 120cm).
- Iron the back piece flat and lay the batting on top, followed by the first oblong block. Make sure that the block is parallel with back piece's edge, which has been cut with at least one of the corners at right angles. This is necessary or the runner will go askew as you sew on the other pieces.
- Next, lay block number two with the right side against block number one, pin together and sew through all the layers (block one and two – batting – back piece) with a single ¼in (0.7cm) seam. Press block number two over with the right side up and then sew blocks number three, four, five and so on in the same way. All that then remains is to cut the runner to size and sew on a pretty binding.

Christmas at Home

However you celebrate Christmas, this runner and some place mats in bright festive colours and with huge hearts will put you in the Christmas mood. Why not make one or a few extra for gifts while you're at it?

Black Place Mat

11¾ × 15¾in (30 × 40cm) approximately

Make the mat out of linen, about 12 × 15½in (30 × 40cm). Freehand quilt the mat and sew on an appliqué heart from page 145 using double-sided fusible interfacing. Finish off with a binding.

Red and White Place Mat

11¾ × 15¾in (30 × 40cm) approximately

Sew together a centre piece, 9½ × 12¾in (24 × 32.5cm) and a border, about 1½in wide. Machine sew on the hearts (pattern page 145) with double-sided fusible interfacing and quilt the mat in gently curved lines. Finish off with a binding.

Heart Runner

16½ × 36½in (42 × 93cm)

The runner is made of 4½in (11.5cm) squares. The centre piece of eighteen white squares is made up of nine horizontal rows of two squares each. The border around the centre piece is made up of equally sized squares, in a variety of red-coloured fabrics.

Appliqué three purple hearts (pattern page 145) on both sides of the runner, secured with double-sided fusible interfacing. Machine quilt the runner with gently curved lines, both lengthwise and across. Finish off with a binding.

Chef's Apron

Here are a couple of ideas for simple aprons, with hearts as the only appliqué. The chef is guaranteed to be pleased with this gift.

The black apron (left) has a centre piece with a pocket and appliqué hearts. The striped apron (right) is made of one fabric; I have simply turned one half so that the stripes are horizontal. I have also decorated the apron with a pocket with small appliqué hearts. Both models are made from the same pattern and can easily be varied. Just try your hand! The patterns are on page 143 and the pattern for the hearts is on page 145.

Christmas Runner
17 x 28½in (43.25 x 72.5cm)

I am member of a little group that loves patchwork. One of the ladies proposed a project, namely to use red and light/white fabrics. We could decide which model and blocks ourselves. At our first meeting we brought with us all the fabrics we planned to use in the model and we all had one or more plans as to what we were going to sew. It was interesting to see what we all defined as red and light/white.

The runner is simple to sew and is made up of six horizontal rows of three blocks each. The blocks are called Town Hall Stairs, and can be varied ad infinitum. I sewed my blocks out of a 3in (7.5cm) square in the centre, with two rounds of 1¼in (3cm) wide strips sewn around. Every round is sewn with a different fabric.

At either end of the runner I have added a 3in (7.5cm) wide border. The runner is machine quilted in both diagonal directions with gently curved lines. The binding in dark fabric forms an elegant frame.

4½in (11.4cm)
3in (7.6cm)
1¼in (3.1cm)
6in (15.2cm)

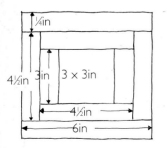

Happy Valentine

11 x 27in (28 x 69cm)

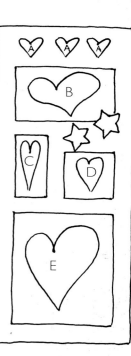

Hearts + love = true. Sew a wall hanging for someone you love and want to delight. If you use strong colours, you will underline the strength of your feelings. Start by quilting a piece of fabric you think is suited as a background for the blocks with hearts. The size of the piece depends on how many and how large, your blocks are. This hanging has a back piece 11 x 27in (28 x 69cm). You can, for instance, quilt the back piece with a diagonal grid system. I recommend you quilt the piece a little larger than you need and cut it to size.

Stitch as follows:

- All the blocks are in different sizes, with different size appliqué hearts (patterns on page 145) fused into place with double-sided fusible interfacing (see page 10).

  Heart A – trace three hearts on to double-sided fusible interfacing and iron them on to the top of the hanging.

  Heart B – trace one heart and fuse it on to a piece of fabric. This is made up of many small patches to a 4½ x 8in (11.5 x 20.5cm) block.

  Heart C – trace one heart and fuse it on to a block measuring 6 x 3in (15 x 7.5cm).

  Heart D – trace one heart on and fuse it on to a block measuring 4½ x 4½in (11.5 x 11.5cm).

  Heart E – trace one heart and fuse it on to a block made up of many patches and measures 9 x 8½in (23 x 21.5cm).

- Cut the heart blocks with pinking shears, or cut in jags with a rotary cutter and place them on the hanging according to your preference (see diagram above). Pin them thoroughly on the hanging and sew them on with a straight seam. Sewing two rounds of straight seams around the blocks gives them a nice look. You can use slightly coarser thread than regular sewing thread, such as silk thread.

- Sew on all the appliqué hearts with two rounds in a straight seam.

- Use the star pattern on page 145 to draw the stars on to double-sided fusible interfacing. Fuse them in place and fasten them with straight seams. Sew on the appliqué hearts at the top of the hanging.

- Sew on a binding and a few brass rings for hanging up the wall hanging – unless the hanging is so large that you need to make a casing for it to hang nicely.

Bag in Cheerful Colours

This colourful bag is perfect for going to your sewing classes or a shopping trip or even a trip to the beach. It is easy to sew and has colourful squares and a black grid intersected with small black and white squares. The bottom is made in a single piece, also in black/white fabric.

Stitch as follows:

- A – cut out thirty-two 3½in (9cm) squares in clear, bright colours.
- B – cut out sixty-four strips for the grid, 3½ x 1½in (9 x 3.75cm) in black.
- C – cut out thirty squares, 1½in (3.75cm) in black and white fabrics.
- Cut out fabric for the bag's bottom in a black and white fabric, 5½ x 17½in (14 x 44.5cm).

- Arrange all the patches in accordance with the diagram (left) and sew them together with a seam allowance of ¼in (0.7cm).
- Cut a piece of fabric for the bag's inside and a piece of stiff batting (wadding) in the same size (so the bag will be stiff enough to stand up).
- Machine quilt the bag freehand. You can use slightly thicker thread than normal for quilting to highlight the seam and make it more decorative. Black thread is a good choice for this.
- Sew both sides of the bag together, remembering to cut it to size first.
- Sew in a strip for decoration in both side seams. Cut this to 1 x 14½in (2.5 x 37cm) and iron it double lengthwise before sewing it into the side seam. One of the sides on my bag has a red strip and the other side has a green one.

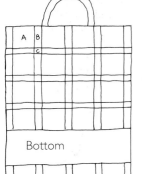

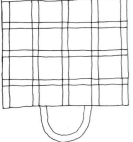

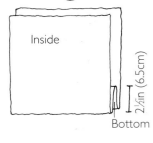

Bottom:

- The bottom is made by folding up the fabric between the side seams and sewing it into the side seams (see diagram on page 54): place the bag with right sides together with the strips fastened with pins on both sides.
- Next, fold the bottom fabric up between the bag's sides. The pleat should be about 2½in (6.5cm) deep. Sew the side seams, using a seam allowance of ¼in (0.7cm). You can either zigzag across the seam or cover the seam with a strip of fabric. Cut the fabric to 1¾in (4.5cm) and sew it into the side seams, together with the pleat. Next, fold it over the seam's raw edges and sew it by hand.
- Along the bag's top edge, you can sew on a 1½in (3.75cm) wide strip inside. Place it with the right side facing the bag's inside and machine sew it on, about ¼in (0.7cm) from the edge.
- Fold the strip on to the bag's outside and machine sew it on.
- If you want a slightly stiffer bottom for the bag, lay a loose piece of cardboard into the bottom. You can cover it with fabric by sewing a pocket that is slightly larger than the piece of cardboard. Lay the piece in the pocket and fold in the opening.

Handles:

- Cut out two pieces of fabric, about 18 x 3in (46 x 7.5cm), two pieces of batting (wadding) 18 x 1½in (46 x 3.75cm) and two strips for the raw edge 18 x 1½in (46 x 3.75cm).
- Fold the fabric in two lengthwise and iron and place the batting between the two layers. Sew a seam, about ¼in (0.5cm) from the edge on both handles.
- Fold the strips in two and sew them as a bias binding over the handles' raw edges.

Cornets

Sew a cornet, fill it with chocolate or some other goodies and give a friend a present next time you are visiting. If she is worried about her figure, just fill the cornet with something fragrant instead! The cornets are easy to sew, so once you have got your sewing machine out you might as well make several.

Stitch as follows:

- Using the measurements on the diagram (right), cut out a paper pattern. I made the cornets in two sizes and both are double.
- Following the pattern, cut out four triangles and sew two and two together along the upper edge.
- Press out the seams and lay them together, right side to right side. This will now look like a narrow triangle.
- Sew a seam all the way around, but leave an opening so you can turn the cornet inside out.
- Turn the cornet inside out through the opening and machine sew the opening closed.
- Place one of the triangles inside the other and press gently.
- Put sweets or something fragrant inside and tie with a silk ribbon.

8in
(20.3cm)

12in
(30.4cm)
or 17in
(43.2cm)

From the Heart

22 x 68in (56 x 172.5cm)

I made this hanging a long time ago and it is a little unusual, both with regard to design and colour. The heart design is simple and the colourful fabrics in the background can be varied according to personal taste. I was also inspired to make a sponge bag.

Stitch as follows:
- Cut out 8in (20.25cm) squares in bright single-coloured fabrics to form the background for the hearts.
- Use the template here to create the heart shapes. Fasten the appliqué hearts using double-sided fusible interfacing (see page 10) and use a zigzag seam for your appliqué seam, preferably with black thread.
- Cut each block in two through the centre and swap the halves around, so they are all lying next to a different colour.
- Sew together two half blocks to a whole one, with overlapping seam allowances – about ½in (1.25cm). You can use black thread to sew them together with two straight seams.
- Cut the blocks to size and sew them together in rows: five rows with three blocks and four rows with two blocks, plus an extra half block.
- Machine quilt the hanging with a zigzag seam and black thread. Quilt it so that the seams are paralleled by vertical and horizontal lines. When I reach a heart, I stop the quilting seam, adjust the sewing machine to a straight seam, sew across the heart, stop and re-adjust the machine to zigzag before continuing to the next heart and so on.
- Finish off with a binding.

Sponge Bag

I had several blocks left over from the From the Heart hanging so I made a matching sponge bag. I added some rectangles around the blocks and used the large sponge bag pattern on page 144.

Descending Angels

We all need an angel once in a while, both visible and invisible. We will leave the invisible ones hovering where they are, but let the visible ones descend on this hanging. They are so pretty they can stay there all year long.

Stitch as follows:

- A – cut out six 6½in (16.5cm) squares in light blue fabrics. These will be the backgrounds for the angels.

- B – cut out twelve 6½ × 2in (16.5 × 5cm) rectangles in red fabrics.
- C – cut out nine red and nine blue squares, 5 × 5in (13 × 13cm). Iron the squares together, right side to right side, one red to one blue, making up nine in total. Pencil up the horizontal, vertical and both diagonal lines on the light fabric.
- Sew on both sides of the diagonal lines, with a seam allowance of ¼in (0.7cm).
- Gently iron and then cut along the horizontal, vertical and both diagonal lines. Press the triangles apart with the seam allowances towards the darkest fabric.

paper on the fabric's wrong side and pull the thread so the seam allowance gathers around the paper. Fasten the thread and press the gathers with an iron. Take out the paper, put batting (wadding) beneath the head and fasten it on to the angel by hand.

■ All the angels have different hair-styles — hemp hair, sheep's wool hair and hair made of machine seams. Be your own hairdresser and create fantasy hairdos! Don't forget to sew on a little ring on each angel's hair — after all, every angel needs its halo.

Block one — three pieces

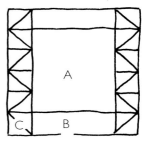

■ The hanging is machine quilted with metallic thread. First, I quilted gently curved lines with the upper feed dog on and then freehand quilted circles, using the free-motion quilting foot. The hanging is finished with a blue binding.

Block two — three pieces

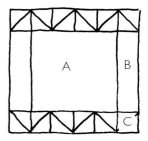

■ Cut the squares to size, 2 x 2in (5 x 5cm).
■ Sew together A, B and C as in the diagram (right), giving three pieces of block one and three pieces of block two. The blocks are actually identical, but block two is rotated 90°.
■ Cut out the fabric you want for the angels using the patterns on pages 142 and 143, and sew them on using double-sided fusible interfacing (see page 10).
■ Cut out the angels' heads on paper, then cut out the heads in fabric with a small seam allowance, just below ¼in (0.7cm), and sew small running stitches along the edge of the seam allowance. Place the

C

59

Sort of Amish
45½ x 82in (115.5 x 208cm)

This quilt was my first using only single-coloured fabrics and grew out of an attempt to set my sewing room in order. I had stored strips of single-coloured fabrics in shoe boxes and was left with the choice of chucking all the boxes and their contents, or making something from these single-colour strips. It was an easy choice and the road to a new bedspread proved short.

Stitch as follows:
- Sew together 1½ x 4in (4 x 10cm) strips to blocks measuring 4 x 14in (10 x 35.5cm), with seam allowance.
- Put the strip blocks together with fabric pieces that have the same measurements as the blocks.
- There are twenty-three strip blocks and twenty-two single-pieces blocks in the bedspread. The first blue border is 1½in (4cm) wide; the broad dark border is 6½in (16.5cm) wide; and the corner squares are 6½ x 6½in (16.5 x 16.5cm).
- Machine quilt the spread with a pattern stitch using green thread, about ⅜in (1cm) from both sides of the seams. The vertical / horizontal quilt line is at an angle of 60° to the frame.
- Finish off the spread with a nice green binding.

Blanket for Dollie
17½ x 22in (44.5 x 56cm)

Do you know a little girl who desperately needs a blanket for her dollie and do you happen to have some strip blocks left over from your Sort of Amish quilt? If so, making a little blanket for the doll is only a few hours' work and is sure to be much appreciated!

After sewing Sort of Amish I was left with two strip blocks. I cut these lengthwise, giving me more, narrower blocks. I then sewed them together with strips that I had cut out measuring 1in (2.5cm) wide. I sewed a 1in (2.5cm) strip around the centre piece, followed by a 4in (10cm) red border, with mauve 4in (10cm) squares in each corner.

I then quilted the whole blanket diagonally, i.e. from corner to corner on the centre piece, with parallel lines about 2in (5cm) apart. Finally, I added a dark binding to round off the blanket. The blanket was such a success that it was with some difficulty I succeeded in getting it away from dollie to send it off to the photographer!

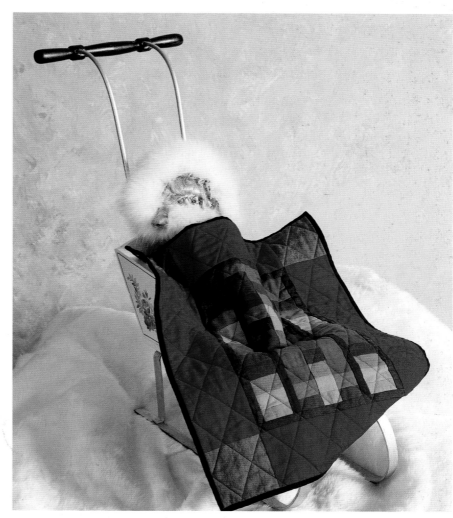

Elsa's Coffee Break

30½ x 49in (77.5 x 124.5cm)

For a while I held many courses in Sweden and got to know many people, leading to renewed visits and new ideas. One of these people was Elsa Petersson in Ørebro, one of the initiators of the quilting association in Ørebro. This gentle and inspiring lady participated at one of my courses in Ørebro and invited me to her home to see the quilts she'd made. Nothing could have made an impassioned quilter like me happier. I fell in love with one of her blankets in particular. It was from the 1950s and sewn out of old clothes and remnants. I had seen the block design used many times before but it hadn't caught my attention. This time was different. Elsa's blanket inspired me and I sewed a blanket of old fabrics. These fabrics were given me by a Norwegian lady – called Else, of all names. I am therefore especially pleased to be able to present this blanket.

Stitch as follows:

- Cut out 1½in (4cm) strips, about 7½in (19cm) long. The measurements are a little generous in order to give you an extra allowance for when you cut out the blocks.
- Sew together three strips and cut them into 3½ x 3½in (9 x 9cm) blocks. Each set of strips gives two blocks. The blanket consists of 140 blocks.
- Arrange the blocks, with horizontal and vertical blocks alternating. The blanket is made up of fourteen horizontal rows of ten blocks each.
- The quilt has a 3in (7.5cm) border on both short sides and each border is made of a different fabric. The borders are made of remnants.
- Machine quilt the blanket diagonally in both directions.
- Finish the quilt with a binding made of remnants, in two different fabrics.

On A White Garden Bench...

At home, there is a multicoloured runner made of sample strips which my fabric club Stoffimport has sent me. The rug is 14½in (37cm) wide and 42in (106.5cm) long.

Stitch as follows:

- For one block, cut out six light and seven dark strips, 1½ x 3in (4 x 7.5cm).
- Sew a light strip on to a dark strip. Finger press. Sew on a light strip. Finger press. Sew on a dark strip. And so on ...
- Cut the 'braided' fabric to size, 3in (7.5cm) wide.
- Sew a light triangle on to the braid's dark side. For the triangle, cut a 7in (18cm) square diagonally.
- Sew a dark triangle on to the braid's light side. To make the triangle, cut a 6in (15.5cm) square diagonally.
- Cut the block to 7½ x 7½in (19 x 19cm). Don't worry if your blocks' measurements differ slightly.
- Sew four and four blocks together, with the dark triangles facing each other and giving you three equally large, new blocks.
- Sew together the three new, large blocks into a runner.
- Machine quilt the runner with a pattern stitch. You can use a multicoloured thread if you want to.
- Finish off the runner with a binding.

Braid

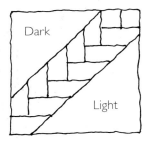

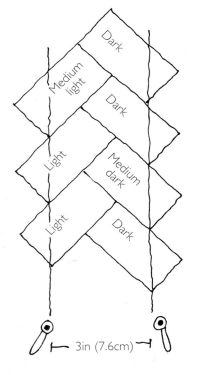

Mother Bag

Stitch as follows:

- Cut out eight 6in (15cm) squares.
- Cut out four 2½in (6.25cm) squares.
- Cut out twelve 6 × 2½in (15 × 6.25cm) rectangles.
- Sew the patches together to a single piece, with two horizontal rows of four squares and with the rectangles and the small squares in between.
- Quilt the piece using a decorative stitch if you want.
- Cut the entire piece to size lengthwise, to 30in (76cm). Remember to leave about ¾in (2cm) of the lining on one of the short sides.
- After sewing the bag into a cylinder shape, you can fold the extra lining over double and sew it by hand in order to cover the seam.
- The bag has a circular bottom with a radius of 4¾in (12cm). You can use two layers of stiff batting (wadding) for the bottom and insert a layer of thick interfacing. Make the bottom a little larger than the actual bag base and quilt it diagonally in both directions, before cutting it to size to fit the base.
- Sew the bottom on to the bag, wrong sides together (insides together) and cover the seam with a 1½in (4cm) wide binding.
- Sew a 1½in (4cm) binding on to the bag's top edge.
- Sew the handles double, with batting inside, with final measurements of 1½ × 24½in (3.5 × 62cm). For a simple way of doing this, see page 102.
- Add a little piece of fabric at either end of the handle, 1½in × 2½in (4 × 6.5cm), fold it double over the raw edges and hand sew it.
- Fasten the handles with buttons on the front, about 1¼in (3cm) below the bag's upper edge.

◀ *This bag is mother to the bag on page 78. See above for assembly instructions.*

Serviettes

Serviettes are very simple to make. Buy some tea towels, fold over one third of the towel and sew the sides together to form a pocket. Divide the pocket with three extra seams. Fasten a cord on to the middle of the towel. After your picnic, place used cutlery in the pockets, roll up the serviette and tie.

Frayed Edges

A while ago I was in the USA. I had been told that the big shops had huge selections of fabrics and state-of-the-art tools, so I had better get ready. Although I wasn't actually going there to shop for patches, obviously I had to have a peek at one of the houses of fabrics. The shop was full of ready-made quilts and I soon spied a quilt with the seams on the right side, cut up and frayed. I ended up with five small patches, a fabric brooch and a burning desire to sew in the frayed-edge technique I'd seen. (See also the projects on pages 13–18.)

Frayed-Edge Quilt

Once safe and sound at home and still full of inspiration, I sewed this quilt. I got out all my brushed cotton fabrics and finished off the quilt in no time at all. Next, I tried the technique with regular cotton fabrics and made a set of cushions for the wicker chair and a frayed bag, all of them in bright and cheerful colours. The quilt is made of sixty-three blocks, in nine horizontal rows of seven blocks each.

Stitch as follows:

- Cut 126 squares out of the fabric, 9in (23cm) each.
- Cut the cotton batting (wadding) into sixty-three squares, 6¾in (17.25cm) each.

Stitch as follows for 31 blocks:

- Lay two squares on top of each other, wrong sides together and trace both diagonal lines with a pencil.
- Remove the upper square, lay a batting (wadding) square on to the centre of the lower square and replace the upper square.
- Pin together the three layers, consisting of fabric, batting and fabric.
- Machine quilt along the diagonal lines.

Stitch as follows for 32 blocks:

- Place two squares exactly on top of each other, wrong sides together.
- Remove the upper square, lay a batting (wadding) square on to the centre of the lower square and replace the upper square.
- Cut out the heart, using the heart pattern on page 148 and place it on the centre of the square.
- Quilt on the heart through all the three layers, using a zigzag seam.
- Lay the blocks back to back and sew together with 1in (2.5cm) seam allowances. Press seams open.
- Cut up the seam allowances, about every ¾–1in (2–2.5cm).
- Finally, machine wash the quilt; you can also tumble dry it a little. Wash the quilt inside a sewn-up duvet cover, otherwise the loose threads may block your washing machine drain. You can tumble dry the quilt without the duvet cover.

Frayed-Edge Cushions

I have sewn these wonderfully bright cushions in two different sizes using the frayed-edge technique described on the previous page.

Stitch as follows for the large cushion:

- A – cut out twelve squares, 6in (15cm) each, in the fabrics you want on the cushion's outside and twelve for the cushion's inside.
- You also need twelve squares of cotton batting (wadding), 3¾in (9.5cm).
- B – cut up eight rectangles, 6 x 14in (15 x 35.5cm) each, in the fabrics you want on the cushion's outside and eight for the rectangles inside.
- You also need eight rectangles of cotton batting, 3¾ x 11¾in (9.5 x 30cm).
- Sew the cushions (see diagram above), using the frayed-edge technique (see previous page).
- Assemble the cushion by sewing on a back piece with the opening/closing you prefer, with a straight seam around the edges. Use the same seam allowance when sewing the blocks together, 1in (2.5cm)
- Cut up the seam allowances, about every ¾–1in (2–2.5cm).
- Wash the cushion in the washing machine, following the washing instructions given for the quilt on the previous page; you can also tumble dry the cushion.

Stitch as follows for the small cushion:

- Cut out sixteen squares, 6in (15cm) each, in the fabrics you want on the cushion's outside.
- Cut out sixteen squares, measurements as above, in the fabrics you want on the cushion's inside. This fabric will be visible in the seams on the outside of the cushion.
- Cut sixteen squares of cotton batting (wadding), 3¾in (9.5cm).
- Sew the sixteen squares together in four lines of four using the frayed-edge technique, as above. Cut up the seam allowances, about every ¾–1in (2–2.5cm).
- Assemble and wash this cushion, as for the large one.

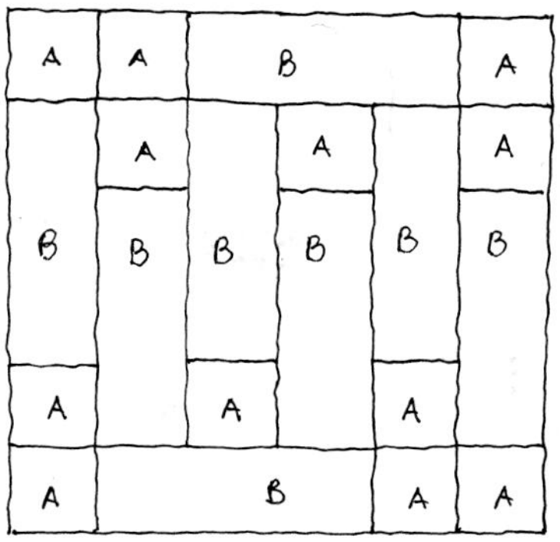

Large cushion layout

Frayed-Edge Bag
16 x 16in (41 x 41cm)

Stitch as follows:

- A – cut up eight squares, 6in (15cm) each, in the fabrics you want on the outside of the bag and eight for the inside of the bag.
- You also need eight squares of cotton batting (wadding), 3¾in (9.5cm).
- B – cut up eight rectangles 6 x 14in (15 x 35.5cm) each, in the fabrics you want on the outside of the bag and eight rectangles for the inside.
- You also need eight rectangles of 3¾ x 11¾in (9.5 x 30cm) cotton batting.
- Sew the bag, using the frayed-edge technique (see previous page).
- Assemble the bag when you have sewn two identical pieces (see diagram overleaf).
- Lay out the pieces facing one another, insides together. Sew a seam on both sides and the bottom, keeping a 1in (2.5cm) seam allowance. It pays to sew a double seam, for reinforcement. You can also sew two rounds along the bag's opening, at 1in (2.5cm) from the edge.
- Sew a seam in each corner of the bottom of the bag. This is done by placing the side seams against the bottom seam; sew the seam about 2¼in (6cm) from the corner.
- Strengthen the bottom by adding a strong piece of cardboard inside a fabric pocket.

Handles:

- Cut out four strips, 3¾ x 33in (9 x 84cm), i.e., two in the fabric you want on the inside of the handle and

two for the handle's outer side. The frayed-edge effect will work best if you select different fabrics for the outer and inner sides of the handles.

■ Cut a 1½ x 33in (4 x 84cm) strip of double-sided fusible interfacing. Place a strip of each fabric, wrong sides together, with the interfacing strip between them and iron together. The interfacing will make the handle stronger and keep the fabrics in place when you sew them together.

■ Fold the handles inwards along the interfacing edges and stitch about ⅜in (1cm) from the folding edge.

■ Machine sew the handles on the inside of the bag.

■ Finally, cut up the seam allowances, a little more closely, about ½in (1.5cm).

■ Wash the bag as described for the quilt on page 69.

Raw and Ready Bags

Here is a new idea for little bags. These are easy to make and you already know the technique from the frayed-edged quilt and cushions on the previous few pages.

Stitch as follows for the Raw is Red bag:

■ Cut out twenty-four squares, 3in (7.5cm), in the fabrics you want on the bag outside.

■ Cut out twenty-four squares, 3in (7.5cm), in the fabrics you want on the bag inside.

■ You also need twenty-four squares of cotton batting (wadding), 1¾in (4.5cm).

■ For the bottom, cut out a 5in (12.75cm) square for the outside and a 5in (12.75cm) square for the inside, as well as a square of batting 3¾in (9.75cm).

■ Lay one inside square and one outside square on top of each other, wrong sides together. Trace both diagonal lines in pencil and place the batting between the two layers. Do this with all twenty-four squares. Repeat for the bottom.

■ Quilt the bottom and all blocks along both diagonals.

■ Sew the bag together in two identical pieces, with three horizontal rows of four squares each. Use ½in (1.25cm) seam allowances with seams on the outside.

■ Cut out two fabric casings, 5 x 9in (12.75 x 23cm).

■ Fold the fabrics for the casings over double and iron

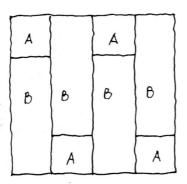

Sew two pieces for the bag

them, wrong sides together and sew them on to the pieces for the bag, with a seam allowance of ½in (1.25cm)

- Sew two stitching lines in the centre of the casing, about ¾in (2cm) apart, for the cord.
- Lay the two pieces for the bag together, insides together and sew them together so they form a cylinder. Start the seam 1½in (4cm) from the casing's upper edge and stop ½in (1.25cm) from the bottom.
- Sew on the bag bottom with the seam allowance on the outside and continue with a seam allowance of ½in (1.25cm).
- Cut up all the seam allowances, about every ½in (1.25cm).
- Wash the bag in the washing machine and pull the cord through to close the bag.

Stitch as follows for the Ready is Black bag:

- Sew four crazy patches blocks, in different shapes. (If you want a small Ready is Black bag, have fairly small blocks.)
- Cut out 1–2½in (2.5–6.5cm) strips, each varying in width and cut on the bias. Judge the width by eye, only using a ruler for straight sewing lines. Cut out the block's centre square without exact measurements and no right angles.
- Sew strips on to two and two sides of the square, and press open seams on the right side. Every time you sew a seam, cut off excess fabric, so you can follow a straight line when sewing.
- Assemble the bag by sewing together the four blocks for the outside. I added a strip on top of and below the blocks once I had

sewn them together because I needed plenty of fabric for the frayed-edge seam allowance.
- Cut out a piece of fabric for the inside in the same size.
- You also need a piece of cotton batting (wadding) of the same size, minus 1¼in (3.25cm) for the length.
- Now place the piece of batting (wadding) between the outer and inner patches, with identical seam allowance above and below.
- Machine quilt the sandwich, only quilting where the batting is, not in the seam allowance.
- Sew together the side seam to form a cylinder. The seam allowance here should be turned inwards and be ¼in (0.7cm).
- Fold the bag double and measure it. This measurement is for the cord casing. Remember to add a

little for the hem.
- Cut out fabric for two casings, 5in (12.75cm) × the measurement you arrived at above. Fold the fabric double and press it, wrong sides together.
- Sew the casing on to the little bag with the seam allowance on the outside, with a seam allowance of ½in (1.25cm).
- Sew two stitching lines on to the middle of the casing, about ¾in (2cm) apart.
- Sew the bottom on with the same seam allowance, on the outside. For the bottom's measurements, take the bag circumference and divide by four.
- Cut up the outward-facing seam allowance ½in (1.25cm) apart.
- Wash the bag in the washing machine and thread in cords for closing it.

73

Vintage Quilt

54½ x 84½in (138.5 x 215cm)

Don't throw out old fabrics; use them for a quilt and see how good they look together. If you quilt piece by piece, you can even use fabric remnants for the back of the quilt.

Stitch as follows for the centre piece:

- Cut out six light and six dark squares, 8in (20.25cm).
- Arrange them together, right sides together, light against dark.
- Trace horizontal, vertical and both diagonal lines with a pencil on the lighter part.
- Sew on both sides of the diagonal lines with a seam allowance of ¼in (0.7cm).

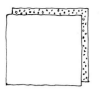

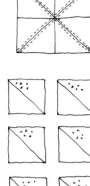

- Gently iron and cut out the horizontal, vertical and both diagonal lines (see diagram).
- Press the triangles apart into a square, with the seam allowance towards one side. Cut the squares to size, 3½in (9cm).
- Sew together four at a time to create twelve blocks, dark triangles next to one another. Arrange the blocks in four horizontal lines, with three blocks in each line.
- The border surrounding the blocks is green, 3½in (9cm) wide. There is a pink square, 3½in (9cm), in each corner.
- The next round consists of thirty light rectangles, 3½ × 6½in (9 × 16.5cm).
- Sew five rectangles on to both long sides and ten rectangles along the shorter edges (in the same direction as the five rectangles, see picture, left).
- Finish off the centre piece with a border of red rectangles. They can be of different lengths, but must all be 3½in (9cm) wide.

Continue stitching as follows:
- Cut out 156 squares for the outer border around the centre piece, each 3½ × 6½in (9 × 16.5cm), in all sorts of colours.
- Sew the patches together, making sure to have dark and light colours alternating and making several sections: two sections for either side (to complete the quilt lengthwise, consisting of eight × three rectangles, a total of forty-eight patches) and four sections for the top and bottom sides (consisting of three × nine rectangles, a total of 108 patches). All rectangles should be placed in an upright position, see picture.
- Machine quilt all seven sections individually.
- Cut all seven quilt sections to size and check that the measurements are correct and identical, so that the sections will fit together when you sew the quilt together.
- Sew the side sections on to either side of the centre piece.
- Take the four identical sections and sew two sections on to both the short sides.
- When sewing the sections together, sew on a strip to cover the seam allowance. Cut the strip to 2in (5cm) wide and a length equivalent to the seam's length. Fold it double and iron, wrong sides together.
- Place the sections to be sewn together right sides together and also place the strip on to the quilt's edge. The strip's raw edges should be placed alongside the sections' raw edges. If you find that the strip is too long, tighten it a bit and cut off the surplus.
- Press the strip so that it covers the seam allowance and everything is quite flat then sew the strip on by hand.
- To finish, sew on the binding. Because you have quilted the spread in sections, there is no need to quilt large areas and your quilt is completed.

The back of the quilt

Cosy Blanket and Pillowcase

Sew a lovely soft blanket made of brushed cotton fabric to wrap around you, or fold the blanket up and put it away inside its pillowcase.

Blanket

49 x 67½in (124.5 x 170cm)

The blanket consists of twenty blocks. Each block is made of four different fabrics – two light coloured and two dark.

Stitch as follows to make one block:

- A – cut out three 3½in (9cm) squares in each of the four fabrics, a total of twelve squares.
- B – cut out one 3⅞in (10cm) square in all four fabrics and cut them into triangles by cutting along the diagonal line.
- Following the diagram, right, arrange the patches in a block before sewing them together, so as to make sure that the fabrics are positioned correctly.
- Sew the twenty blocks and arrange them in five horizontal lines of four patches each. Sew the blocks together.
- Using four fabrics make two borders, measuring 3½ x 12½in (9 x 31.7cm), for the blanket's short sides and sew them on to the blanket, one on either side.
- You can machine quilt the blanket and decorate it with a few buttons if you wish.
- Enclose the blanket with a binding.

Pillowcase

21½ x 33½in (54.5 x 85cm)

Stitch as follows for the case:

- Using remnants from the blanket, sew a centre piece for the pillowcase. This should be about 15½ x 27½in (39.5 x 70cm).
- Using the darkest fabrics, sew a frame around the centre piece, about 3½in (9cm) wide.
- Machine sew on naïve-style flowers – black thread stands out clearly. Use the patterns on pages 146/147, or cut out the flowers without a pattern. Use double-sided fusible interfacing.
- The pillowcase is machine quilted in free-motion, with text and hearts. The text is: 'I am a cosy pillow – made by Lise – for you' but you could use any language.
- Appliqué, quilt and cut to size the front of the pillowcase. Assemble the front to the back by sewing on a binding.
- Machine quilt the back piece – this is the same length as the front piece but narrower, about 3½in (9cm) shorter on both sides.
- Sew ribbons on to the case's back side, for closing the case.

- Sew a binding on the pillowcase front and back pieces at the same time and decorate with buttons.
- Finish off with a seam along the edge of the two longest sides, so the back piece is sewn on properly (see diagram).

For one block:
A – three squares of each fabric
B – one square of each fabric, cut into triangles by cutting along one of the diagonals

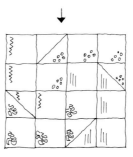

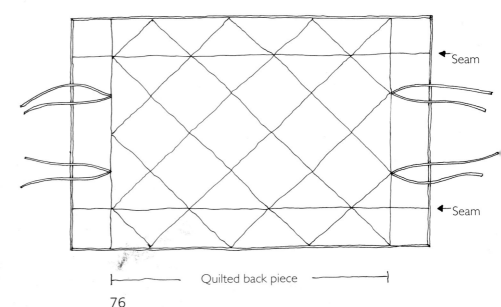

Seam

Seam

Quilted back piece

76

Twins

23¼ × 23¼in (59 × 59cm).

I hold courses on simple shapes with checked (chequered) fabrics. My dear friend Ellen Borge attended one of these courses. She described the fabrics she brought with her to the course as horribly ugly — some of which I had given her! Her intention was to get rid of them and, needless to say, I was to help her.

Although the fabrics were far from beautiful, the result pleased us all. You can see Ellen's cloth on the table and the model on the chair is mine. We quilted the blankets by hand; Ellen used regular quilt stitches and I used a stitch called crow's feet. The cloth is made of a centre piece consisting of six by six blocks; the surrounding border consists of triangles.

Stitch as follows:

- Cut out the pieces for A (see diagram), using 3¾in (9.5cm) squares, cut diagonally. Use your darkest fabrics.
- Cut out the pieces for B, using 2⅜in (6cm) squares, cut diagonally. Use fabrics ranging from light coloured to medium light.
- Cut out the pieces for C, 2in (5cm) squares. Use more of your darkest fabrics.
- Sew together thirty-six blocks, following the diagram and arrange so the large dark triangles face each other, to give a large square, balancing on a corner.
- The border consists of A-type triangles, in the same fabrics as those used for triangle B.
- Quilt the cloth by hand, using the stitch on page 149 or regular quilting stitches.
- Finish with a dark binding.

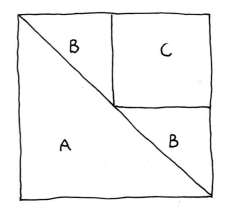

Bags with Hearts

These bags are 'babies' of the bag on page 67. The shape and assembly are identical but the outside design is something quite special.

Stitch as follows:

- Cut out six rectangles, each measuring 4 × 12in (10 × 30cm). You can use two and two rectangles in the same fabric or a different combination.
- Sew in a 2 × 12in (5 × 30cm) strip between the rectangles.
- Sew the pieces together and appliqué the hearts with machine seams (pattern on page 148). Follow the assembly instructions for the mother bag on page 67.

Soft Sewing Bags

Stitch the bags as follows:
A – large oblong green/blue bag with appliqué heart

- The bag's outside is made up of three fabrics. The centre piece is 4 x 12in (10 x 30.5cm) and the two side pieces are 4½ x 12in (11.5 x 30.5cm).
- You can appliqué the heart with machine seams using double-sided fusible interfacing. The heart pattern is on page 148.
- Quilt the piece with batting (wadding) and a fabric that will be on the bag's inside. Use your sewing machine and sew a normal straight seam with upper feed dogs, or try your hand at free-motion quilting.
- Cut the piece to size, 12 x 12in (30.5 x 30.5cm). If you have quilted it closely, the piece may be a little smaller.
- On both of the zip sides, sew on a 2 x 12in (5 x 30.5cm) edge (see diagram). First sew it from the inside, press it over to the right side and fold in the edge to about ¾in (2cm). Sew a stitching line on the very edge of the fold.
- Place a 16in (40cm) zip along the edge and stitch it down with two seams – one as close as possible to the zip itself, the other ³⁄₁₆in (0.5cm) from the first stitching.
- Sew a machine seam across the zip near the short side of the bag to prevent the zip tearing when you cut it off. Cut off the ends of the zip and make sure it runs properly. Open the zip halfway.
- Take a silk ribbon, 1 x 3in (2.5 x 7.5cm) and fold it double. Fasten it with a machine seam so it covers the zip's ends.

- Study the diagram below and fold in two pleats of fabric towards the middle of the bag, about ⅜in (1cm) apart. Sew the seams above the folds and seal the seam in zigzag stitch.
- The bag's inside will look even nicer if you cover the raw edges with a strip or bias binding. Turn the sewing bag inside out and arrange the pleats.

B – large orange bag with appliqué heart and brown bag with triangles

- The orange bag's outside is sewn together from three fabrics. The centre piece is 4 x 12½in (10 x 32cm) and the side pieces are 3½ x 12½in (9 x 32cm).
- You can machine appliqué on the heart using double-sided fusible interfacing (see page 10). See page 148 for the heart pattern.
- The brown bag's outside is made of light and dark triangles N from the Bite of Autumn throw, page 96.
- Follow the instructions for bag A, but cut the piece to 10 x 12½in (25.5 x 32cm) and cut the edge for the zip to 2 x 10in (5 x 25cm). The zip is 12in (30cm) long.

C – oblong pink/turquoise bag and grey silk bag

- The outside is sewn from two pieces of the same size, 4¼ x 8in (11 x 20cm).
- Follow the procedure for bag A, but cut the piece to 8 x 8in (20 x 20cm) and cut the edge for the zip to 1¾ x 8in (4.5 x 20cm). It will be ½in (1.25cm) wide. The zip is 10in (25cm) long.
- You can use a strip of fabric instead of the silk ribbon. If so, cut the fabric to 1½ x 3in (4 x 7.5cm).

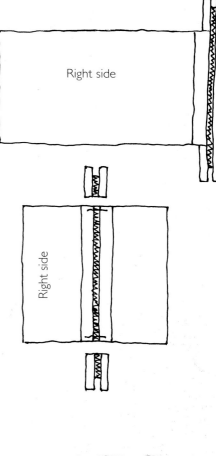

Right side

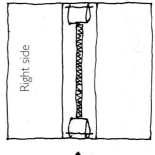

Right side

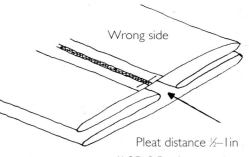

Right side

Silk ribbon

Wrong side

Pleat distance ½–1in (1.25–2.5cm) approximately

Fold it with the raw edges facing the middle, fold it towards the centre and sew it together with stitches as close to the edge as possible.

D – pink bag and small black and pink bag

- The outside of the pink bag is sewn out of a single piece of fabric, 6 × 8in (15 × 20cm). The outside of the black bag is made of two pieces of fabric, both 3¼ × 8in (8.25 × 20cm).
- Follow the instructions for bag A, but cut the piece to 6 × 8in (15 × 20cm) and cut the edge for the zip to 1¾ × 8in (4.5 × 20cm). It will be ½in (1.25cm) wide when finished. The zip is 8in (20cm) long.
- You can use a strip of fabric instead of silk ribbon. Cut the fabric to 1½ × 3in (4 × 7.5cm). Fold it with raw edges facing the middle, fold it again towards the centre and sew it together with stitches very close to the edge.

Simple Checked Quilt

28½ × 28½in (72.5 × 72.5cm)

Checked (chequered) fabrics have always been my favourites. Many of the fabrics in this quilt are from cast-off clothes and fabrics found at jumble sales. I have grouped the fabrics into light, medium and dark shades, regardless of colours. This is a fun way of using fabrics with lots of different colours. If you look closely, you'll see that the star corners are in different colours; so is the background, but using only light shades. The quilt has four stars and its corners make up a fifth star in the centre because of the way the light, medium and dark fabrics are arranged.

Follow the diagram, right, and arrange the entire quilt before sewing it together, so it's easier to see whether you have arranged the fabrics correctly. If you find it difficult to see the difference between light, medium and dark fabrics, try looking through a camera.

Stitch as follows:

- Cut out several light and dark triangles, by cutting 3¾in (9.5cm) squares and cutting them diagonally.
- Arrange the triangles in accordance with the diagram below – try looking through a camera to give you a better view; that way you can see whether the light triangles are joined up and that the darker triangles form the star corners.
- When you have arranged the stars, you can start filling in the four star centres. Use small, 1½in (4cm) squares and arrange them in the squares, four by four. Make sure you use the right seam allowance, ¼in (0.7cm), when sewing together the small squares.
- Once you have sewn the centre squares, sew the triangles on to the sides of the square, using medium-shade triangles. Make sure that the fabrics are of a medium shade compared with the star corners, excepting the centre field, where they should be dark. This is what gives you the fifth star. The frame around the centre is divided into several sections, but can actually be identical on all four sides – it's up to you.
  A – 3½in (9cm) wide.
  B – 2½in (6.5cm) wide.
  C – 1½in (4cm) wide.
- Sew together the whole quilt as in the diagram.
- Quilt the whole work by hand, with about ¼in (0.7cm) distance from the seams.
- Finish off with a binding.

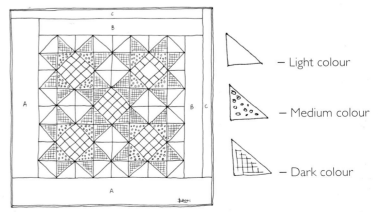

– Light colour

– Medium colour

– Dark colour

Crazy Appliqué

This striking set of appliqué runner, mats and cushions will bring a bright look to your house and garden at any time of year. The appliqué is straightforward and the quilting simple.

Crazy Runner
9½ x 45in (24 x 114cm)

Stitch as follows:

- Cut out ten pieces of fabric in colours that go together. You can use the measurements 8 x 9in (20 x 23cm), or similar.
- Iron double-sided fusible interfacing on to the back of all fabrics. On two of the pieces, draw identical lines, dividing them into ten differently sized patches.
- Tear off the double-sided fusible interfacing paper from the fabrics. Don't throw away the two paper pieces you have drawn on.
- Lay the fabric patches on top of each other, five at a time, wrong side to right side, with the interfacing paper you have drawn on, on top. Cut along each line. These pieces will be your appliqué.
- Cut out a linen runner in the desired size – mine is 9½ x 45in (24 x 114cm)
- Lay out the appliqué pieces and iron them on to the linen where you want them.
- Cut batting (wadding) and backing to the same size as your linen piece.
- Lay the backing, batting and linen on top of one another and pin and tack (baste) together.
- Appliqué the pieces on, sewing through all the layers.
- Gently press the runner and check that it has right angles. Finish off with a binding.

Crazy Mats
12 x 15½in (30 x 40cm)

Stitch as follows:

- Cut out the linen for the place mats in the desired size.
- For four place mats, you will need twenty of the crazy patches you have left over from the runner.
- Iron on five identical appliqué pieces on to each mat, using different fabrics. Appliqué them on using the sewing machine.
- Quilt the place mats with batting (wadding) and backing. For the quilt line, base yourself on shape of the appliqués. If you use dark thread for the quilting, the seam will become part of the appliqué.
- Cut the place mats to size and then sew on a binding.

Crazy Cushions
15 x 15in (38 x 38cm)

Stitch as follows:

- Cut out linen in the size desired for the cushions.
- Lay out the rest of the appliqué shapes to form a flower and machine sew on the appliqués.
- Quilt the cushions diagonally with squares, and across the flowers.
- Cut the cushions to size and lay them on the backing, wrong sides together. Choose a back side for the cushion of your liking.
- To finish, sew on a binding through all layers.

Summer Breeze Tablecloth

40 × 40in (102 × 102cm)

The plan was to sew a pastel tablecloth for my veranda table and to photograph the tablecloth on the table, but time flew and suddenly autumn was upon us. We had to photograph the tablecloth on a different table, in different surroundings. Not that the tablecloth minded, it looks even better here than on my weather-beaten veranda table.

I sewed the tablecloth in pastels of the darkest variety. The border is a densely patterned, fruity fabric. The blocks are made up of the good old Flying Geese design, but with a new twist to the technique. It is well worth a try, but make sure to be precise in your work. The instructions below are for one set of four Flying Geese.

Stitch as follows:

- X – cut out one 5¼in (13.25cm) square.
- Y – cut out four 2⅞in (7cm) squares.
- On the wrong side of all four Y squares, trace diagonal lines.
- Lay two Y squares on top of X squares, right sides together, so that the traced diagonal lines meet.
- Sew on either side of the diagonal, leaving a ¼in (0.7cm) seam allowance.
- Cut along the diagonal line. Press the small triangles away from the large ones.
- Place a Y on each side of the patches, so that the diagonal line goes from the corner to the centre.
- Sew on either side of the diagonal line, leaving a ¼in (0.7cm) seam allowance.
- Cut along the diagonal line. Press the small triangles away from the large one.
- You now have four identical Flying Geese. Sew them together into a row, 4½ × 8½in (11.5 × 21.5cm), see diagram below. On both long sides, sew a strip, 2½ × 8½in (6.5 × 21.5cm). The tablecloth consists of sixteen blocks, with four horizontal, four-block rows. The fruity border is 4½in (11.5cm) wide.
- Machine quilt the tablecloth with a decorative stitch in multicoloured thread.
- To finish, bind the tablecloth in a clear, green fabric.

Large Sponge Bag and Small Make-Up Bag

Flying Geese feature again on these bright bags and the designs suit many types of fabrics – from traditional pastels to funky moderns and stylish retros.

Stitch as follows for a sponge bag or make-up bag:

- Sew together fabric pieces or blocks for the sponge

bag's exterior. You can either pick one of my suggestions, or sew a design of your own.
- Quilt the piece with some stiff batting (wadding) and a piece of fabric in the same size, which will be the bag's inside. The make-up bag does not need such stiff batting.
- Cut the pieces to size.
- Lay the piece with right sides together and sew it together to form a cylinder.
- If you want to hide the side seams, you can sew a strip into the seam. If so, cut a 2in (5cm) wide strip, fold it double, iron it and sew it into the seam. You can sew it down by hand at the end.

- Sew a binding on to the top of the bag. You can cut this to 1½in (4cm) and its length should equal the bag's circumference. Machine sew on the binding, starting on the wrong side.
- Iron on the binding so its raw edge faces the bag's raw edge; fold it over to the right side and sew down with machine stitching.
- To sew the bottom, fold the folds from either side towards the centre, with a space of about 1½in (4cm) for the large bag and about 1in (2.5cm) for the make-up bag. Sew the seam.

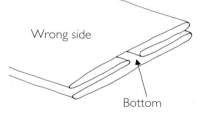

Wrong side

Bottom

Distance between the pleats: arge sponge bag 1½in (4cm); make-up bag 1in (2.5cm)

- You can cover the bottom seam with a strip, like the side seam.
- Turn the bag the right way out.
- The zip has to be the same length as the bag, folded over double. The zip for the sponge bag is 15¾in (40cm) and 7¾in (20cm) for the make-up bag.
- Machine sew the zip on to the right side, but start and stop the seam 4in (10cm) from the edge of the sponge bag and 1½in (4cm) from the edge of the make-up bag.
- Take hold of the edge at the top, where the zip is loose and fold the bag sides into the bag.
- Sew a few stitches where the zip seam starts and stops and into

the pleat that turns in towards the bag. This is to make sure that the bag keeps its shape, both when opened and closed.
- At the ends of the zips, I have sewn on a triangle, bias binding or name tags.
- On the inside of the bag, there will be a pleat on the bottom. You can sew this by hand.
- Cut two 3½ × 12in (9 × 30.5cm) strips for the handles. Fold over the seam allowances at the short ends and sew a stitching line along both outer edges. Fold them lengthwise with the raw edges in towards the centre, so that they are ¾in (2cm) when folded over.
- Fasten the handles with a few seams at the very top of the bag.

Suggestions for the sponge bag's outside:
Blue pastels:
- Sew six sets of Flying Geese, a total of twenty-four pieces.
- Sew together four rows of Flying Geese, six pieces per row, all in the same direction.
- Sew in a piece of fabric, 4½ × 12½in (11.5 × 31.75cm), between each row, a total of four strips.

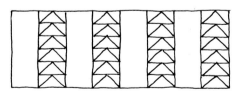

Green and black:
- Cut out four pieces each in two different green fabrics, 4½ × 6½in (11.5 × 16.5cm).
- Arrange them in alternate colours and sew them into a single piece. Also sew two

triangles into the seam, in the centre front and centre back. Make the triangles out of two 2½in (6.5cm) squares, folded twice diagonally.
- Cut out a 6½ × 32½in (16.5 × 82.5cm) piece in black fabric and then sew it underneath the eight first pieces.
- After quilting and assembling the sponge bag, sew on a button on both the loose triangles.

Yellow, brown and black:
- Sew eight sets of Flying Geese, resulting in thirty-two pieces – of which you will only use twenty-four. (Each set will leave you one to spare.)
- Sew together three and three Flying Geese to eight rows, all heading in the same direction.
- Sew a piece of fabric – 4½ × 6½in (11.5 × 16.5cm) – on to the bottom of each row of fabric to form an oblong block.
- Sew together all the blocks in the same direction. You can also add a 1in (2.5cm) strip, pressed double, between each block to become a decorative edge.

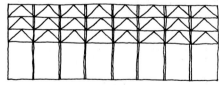

Black make-up bag:
This is sewn from a piece of fabric 16 × 6in (41 × 15.5cm). It can be made with or without appliqué. The heart pattern is on page 148.

'Bobbins' Throw

52 × 69½in (132 × 176cm)

The back of the throw

Sometimes the sewing room needs tidying up. Once in a while things are thrown out to make space for new purchases. Two baskets full of fabrics from old flannel shirts had stood undisturbed for a long time. I could not bring myself to throw them out, but decided to try to make some sort of throw. All the fabrics were clean and had been cut and ironed, so it was only a question of cutting out and sewing.

The fabrics used in these shirts are often in a loose weave and not suited to blocks with small patches. The patches had to be quite large and I decided that a bobbin block would be suitable. To make the block look like a bobbin, I needed a small triangle that could represent the thread. Because I didn't want the triangle to be too small, I folded a square and sewed it in while sewing the seam. When I had finished the throw, there wasn't much left of the old shirts, but what there was I used for the backing and the remainder of the fabrics were sent off to Denmark with a fellow quilter. Sharing with friends feels great.

Stitch as follows to make two blocks:

- Cut out two 9½in (24cm) squares in two different fabrics. One of the squares will be the 'bobbin' and the other the background. If you lay the squares on top of one another when you cut them along both diagonal lines, you will have four identical triangles in each fabric.
- Arrange them in two blocks, making sure there are two and two identical triangles in each block (see picture detail below).
- Cut out four 3in (7.5in) squares. Fold them diagonally, wrong sides together, to form a triangle and iron.
- Lay the triangles so that they will be included in the seam when you sew. Make sure that they are facing the right way on top of the background fabric. Press seams apart if your fabrics are thick.
- Quilt each block separately, using batting (wadding) and backing, cut to 9½in (24cm) squares.
- Cut the blocks to identically sized 8¾in (22cm) squares.
- You need forty-eight blocks. Lay them out in opposite directions, in eight rows of six blocks each.

Front

Back

95

- When sewing blocks together, sew in a strip on the back to cover the seam allowances (see picture bottom of page 95).
- Cut the strips to 2in (5cm), fold them over and iron them wrong sides together. The strips should be the same length as the seam you are to sew. It is a good idea to cut the strip to the right size before sewing them together.
- Lay the blocks together, right sides together and lay the strip edge to edge with the blocks. The strips' raw edge should be alongside the blocks' raw edge. You may feel that the strip is a little too long. If so, tighten the strip slightly and cut off surplus.
- Press the strip so it covers the seam space and all lies flat, then sew the strips on by hand.
- Sew the blocks together with a strip, first one by one, two by two, four by four and so on.
- To prevent the seam from becoming too thick, the strip has been sewn so that the seams fold over in opposite directions. This is done by placing the strips on top when sewing together two blocks; when sewing the next two blocks, the strip is placed beneath the blocks when sewing. See the picture of the back of the throw on page 95 for position of strips.
- Finish off the throw with a binding – and voilà, it is done!
- Make yourself comfortable in your easy chair, wrap the throw around your knees and watch a film. If the film gets too exciting, instead of biting your nails, simply grab hold of the loose triangles.

Bite of Autumn Throw

62½ x 90in (159 x 229cm)

Several years ago I bought a set of rulers called Pandora's box. The box was full of rulers in different shapes and sizes. I have used two of the triangles from this set in my Bite of Autumn throw. If you happen to have this set of rulers, use the P and N triangles. If you have to make templates yourself, trace my diagrams on page 149.

Each block requires: one large P triangle and nine N triangles. Every alternate block has four light and five dark N triangles and every other block has five light and four dark N triangles. The diagram on page 149 shows what the blocks look like, separately and joined up.

Lay out all four block rows, following the picture opposite. Between each row and on the short sides, you need more light and dark N triangles. Lay them out in the order you want them, with alternating dark and light triangles and sew the quilt together.

Bite of Autumn was quilted with repeated flower rows by a quilting company and when it returned I sewed a dark purple binding on.

Piecemeal Blanket

51½ x 68½in (131 x 174cm)

A blanket for cool, dark evenings, in light, delicate colours, is perfect for wrapping around your legs. These colours will let you go on feeling the clear, warm days of the summer for a long time after summer is over. The blanket is made of brushed cotton and is easy to sew. The quilting is simple too: quilt each block before sewing the blanket together. The blanket is built up of 4½in (11.5cm) squares. The borders are 1¾in (4.5cm) wide strips. Use a seam allowance of ¼in (0.7cm) for all seams.

Stitch as follows:

- Start by sewing together twelve blocks, following the diagram below and distributing the red/yellow colours among six of the blocks and the blue/green colours among the other six. The strips are very light, almost white. Each block is machine quilted with batting (wadding) and a backing and all blocks are cut to the same size.
- Lay out the blocks, with red/yellow and blue/green alternating on a board or on the floor – this will help you keep track of which blocks go where.
- Sew the blocks together with a binding by first cutting a 1½in (4cm) wide strip. Lay the blocks back to back in pairs, with the strip alongside the blocks and sew them together with a single seam.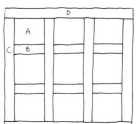
- Fold and press the strips over the resulting raw edges and sew it neatly by hand. This will be like sewing the binding in a single fabric and will look like a rouleau on the blanket's right side. It's a good idea to use a visible colour.
- Go on sewing the blocks together two and two at a time, four and four and so on until all the blocks have been sewn together.
- Finish the blanket with a binding.

Country Walk Blanket

33½ x 67in (85 x 170cm)

Years ago, almost everybody sewed hexagons around cardboard templates that could be bought ready-made, in all sizes. I bought my share of templates but my hexagons continue to be stored away, with fabrics tacked on to them. I therefore had more than enough hexagons for this blanket. My hexagons are not very large, 1½in (4cm) from corner to corner. I sewed them together into eight flowers, of seven hexagons each. I used cast-off clothes and few new fabrics but all were checked (chequered), with plenty of blue.

Stitch as follows:

- Cut out forty-four 6in (15cm) squares in blues. Some can have a tiny bit of red in them. Arrange them in eleven horizontal rows of four squares each.
- Cut out lighter 6in (15cm) squares for the surrounding border. Of the twenty-eight pieces you need, you have to cut up six squares to form twelve 3 x 6in (7.5 x 15cm) rectangles.
- Arrange the squares on the long side, the rectangles on the short side and decorate every other square on the long side with a hexagonal flower. You can sew them on either by hand or machine, but remember to take out the cardboard templates.
- You can machine quilt the blanket with diagonal lines; I used a red silk thread.
- Add a binding to finish.

Country Bag

16½ x 19in (42 x 49cm)

If you are going for a country walk, you will need something to carry the blanket in. I sewed the bag in the same fabrics as the blanket.

Stitch as follows:

- Cut out eighteen 6in (15cm) squares. Sew the squares together, three horizontal rows of six squares each.

Christmas Tablecloth

35½ x 35½in (90 x 90cm)

You can start off using the tablecloth on the table and then move it to underneath the Christmas tree when Christmas really gets going.

Stitch as follows:

- Cut thirty-six squares of red/white checked fabrics, 5½ x 5½in (14 x 14cm). Cut a red square 3 x 3in (7.5 x 7.5cm) for each of the corners. You will also need red fabric for the border, 3in (7.5cm) wide.
- Sew the tablecloth squares together and add the border and corner squares.
- Trace twelve trees, twelve pots, twelve trunks and twelve stars (patterns on pages 150 and 151) on to double-sided fusible interfacing (the paper side). Cut out all designs, making sure to leave a little space outside the pencilled design. Iron them on with the adhesive side to the fabric's wrong side and then cut them out on the pencilled line.
- Pull off the paper from the designs and iron them on to the tablecloth in the positions indicated on the photograph. All the designs were then machine stitched on using embroidery thread.
- Machine quilt the tablecloth with a straight seam.
- Finish with a dark red binding.

Gift for the Dressmaker

Stitch as follows:

- Cut out twenty-three squares in red or brown fabric and twenty-two squares in light fabrics, all 1½ × 1½in (4 × 4cm) for the flap.
- Sew them together, with red/brown and light shades alternating, with five horizontal rows of nine patches each. Cut out a piece of fabric, 9½ × 10½in (24 × 26.75cm), to match the colour of the flap and sew it on to the flap.
- When the kit is finished, quilt the entire piece with batting (wadding) and a fabric that will be on the inside. You can make the quilting lines slightly curved if you like.
- Make a pocket by quilting together two pieces of fabric with batting in between 6 × 9½in (15.25 × 24cm). Cut two 1½ × 9½in (4 × 24cm) strips, one for the pocket and one for the case's short side. Sew the strips on to the case as a binding, making sure they cover the raw edges. Refer to the diagram for positioning the pocket, and sew it on to the kit itself, with a seam along the lower edge and a seam forming an extra pocket.
- Sew a 1½in (4cm) binding around the three remaining sides. If you want to include a buttonhole loop, sew it on at the same time. Using a 1½ × 3in (4 × 7.5cm) strip, make a loop. Fold the strip of fabric over double, twice, so it is about ⅜in (1cm) wide. Sew on a button that matches the loop.
- If you have a nice-looking tag, sew it on with some batting underneath, so it can double as a pincushion.

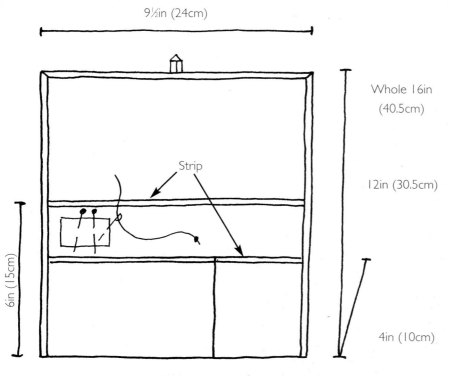

9½in (24cm)

Whole 16in (40.5cm)

12in (30.5cm)

4in (10cm)

6in (15cm)

Strip

115

Festive Runner, Place Mats and Cushion

I have used the same block for this runner, four place mats and cushion (overleaf). The difference is the block size. The runner and place mat blocks are the same size, but the one for the cushion I made a little bigger. I chose red and light fabrics, but the models look just as good in different colours – what about using some remnants?

Festive Runner

12½ x 36½in (31.5 x 92.5cm)

Stitch as follows:

- Cut out and sew together six blocks, following the first diagram below, with A, D and E being red fabrics and B and C being light fabrics = a red block.
- Cut out and sew together six blocks, following the diagram, with A, D and E being light fabrics and B and C being red fabrics = a light block.
- Sew together four and four blocks to form three large blocks, with alternating red and light blocks. Finally, sew together the three big blocks.
- Free motion quilt the runner with a heart pattern seam on the machine.
- Complete the runner with a dark red binding.

Runner measurements:
A – 2 x 2in (5 x 5cm)
B – 2 x 2in (5 x 5cm)
C – 3½ x 2 (9 x 5cm)
D – 3½ x 3½in (9 x 9cm)
E – 3½ x 6½in (9 x 16.5cm)

Cushion measurements:
A – 2½ x 2½in (6.25 x 6.25cm)
B – 2½ x 2½in (6.25 x 6.25cm)
C – 4½ x 2½in (11.5 x 6.25cm)
D – 4½ x 4½in (11.5 x 11.5cm)
E – 4½ x 8½in (11.5 x 21.5cm)

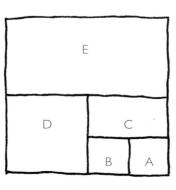

One block

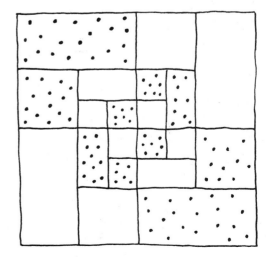

Four blocks

117

Festive Cushion

16½ × 16½in (42 × 42cm)

Stitch as follows:

- Cut out two red and two light blocks and sew as for the runner.
- Free-motion quilt the cushion with a heart pattern and attach a back piece when sewing the binding on to the cushion. You can close it either with buttons or some other closing device.

Festive Place Mat

12½ × 12½in (31.5 × 31.5cm)

Stitch as follows:

- Cut out and sew as for the runner. Each mat is made up of two red and two light blocks.
- I have free motion quilted them like the runner and added a red binding to finish.

Small Mat

9¼ × 13in (23.5 × 33cm)

If you want smaller measurements than the ones on page 117, here are the measurements for a little place mat. You can use it to decorate a small table or to line a bread basket.

Small mat measurements:
A – 1 × 1in (2.5 × 2.5cm)
B – 1 × 1in (2.5 × 2.5cm)
C – 1 × 1½in (2.5 × 4cm)
D – 1½ × 1½in (4 × 4cm)
E – 1½ × 2½in (4 × 6.25cm)

Christmas Throw for the Easy Chair

48 x 72in (122 x 183cm)

*I sewed this throw in colours
that remind me of Christmas:
purple, red, dark orange,
cerise and light, light colours,
reminding me of snow. The
finished blocks are 12 x 12in
(30.5 x 30.5cm).*

Stitch as follows to make
one block:

- Cut out eight dark and eight light
  squares, 3½ x 3½in (9 x 9cm). Sew
  them together with alternating
  dark and light squares, to form a
  square block of four horizontal
  rows of patches, with four
  patches each. If you prefer sewing
  the patches together more
  quickly, cut out 3½in (9cm) strips,
  sew them together two by two
  (one dark and one light) and cut
  up to 3½in (9cm) pieces. Lay
  them on top of one another, dark
  next to light and then sew them
  together into blocks of four. You
  will need four blocks of four for
  one large block. Sew a total of
  twenty-four blocks, each with six
  horizontal rows of four rows.
- Machine quilt the throw
  diagonally, with gently curved
  lines, in purple thread.
- Finish off with a binding.

Cute Tablecloth with Hearts

45½ x 45½in (115.5 x 115.5cm)

I had initially planned to use this tablecloth on a round table, with the hearts lying just on the edge – but it looks very good on a square table too. I sewed the cloth from identically sized squares and have added the hearts for decoration.

Stitch as follows:

- Cut out 226 squares in light fabrics, such as pink, pale yellow, beige and pale green; thirty olive squares and sixty-eight moss green squares.
- Lay out the light squares for a centre block, fourteen by fourteen pieces, followed by a round of alternating light and olive squares and a round of moss green squares. The tablecloth is now composed of eighteen by eighteen squares. Sew the squares together.
- Now machine quilt the whole tablecloth with straight vertical and horizontal seams.
- Appliqué on the hearts (pattern on page 152) using double-sided fusible interfacing and straight seams, as described for the advent wall hanging on page 108.
- Finish the tablecloth with a dark green binding.

Christmas Hearts

Red Tea Cosy

Stitch as follows:

- Sew together three different fabrics, 4½ x 10½in (11.5 x 27cm) for both sides of the cosy.
- Quilt both sides together with batting (wadding) and backing (for the inside).
- Using the tea cosy pattern (page 151), lay the pattern on the ready-quilted patches and cut out in accordance with the pattern.
- Using the hearts from the pattern on page 152, appliqué on the hearts, positioning them as on the photograph. Adjust your sewing machine to a straight seam or a narrow zigzag, attach the embroidery foot, remove the feed dog and sew around each design two or three times freehand. The seams do not need to be exactly on top of one another. Sew the seams about ⅛in (3mm) from the edge. This will give you visible raw edges around the hearts and visible appliqué seams on the inside of the cosy.
- Sew and quilt the fabric for the tea cosy pleat (gusset) – the finished measurement of this, when quilted, should be 3 x 28½in (7.5 x 72.5cm).
- Sew all three pieces together with the seam allowance sticking out – use a seam allowance of ¼in (0.7cm).
- Sew on a 1½in (4cm) wide strip for the binding around the two curved lines and finally a strip around the bottom edges.
- Fasten a loop with a button on top of the tea cosy. Using a strip 2 x 6in (5 x 15.25cm), make a loop by folding it over twice, to a width of about ½in (1.25cm).

Black Tea Cosy

Stitch as follows:

- If you've made the Christmas hearts wall hanging (overleaf) and have a block left over, use that – or make a new block by cutting out a 4½ x 8½in (11.5 x 21.5cm) rectangle in grey fabric.
- Cut out 1½in (4cm) strips and sew them on three sides of the block, in two rounds of different fabrics. Continue with another fabric, so that the piece is large enough for the tea cosy pattern (page 151).
- Quilt the entire piece with batting (wadding) and backing for the inside and fasten on an appliqué heart (pattern on page 152), as for the red tea cosy, but instead of using straight seams on the raw edges, fasten the heart with large freehand zigzag movements.
- Quilt a piece the same size for the tea cosy's other side and cut out both using the pattern.
- Make up the black cosy as described for the red one.

Christmas Hearts Wall Hanging

16½ x 28½in (42 x 72.5cm)

Stitch as follows:

- Cut out nine rectangles, 4½ x 8½in (11.5 x 21.5cm) in various grey fabrics. Choose a fairly light grey, otherwise the hanging will look too dull.
- Sew them together in three rows of three patches each.
- Add a border, using 1½in (4cm) strips. Use red, light and almost white fabrics and some that are both red and white.
- Machine quilt the wall hanging with gently curved lines, vertically and horizontally.
- Appliqué on the hearts (pattern on page 152) in different red and cerise fabrics on to the grey rectangles, as outlined for the red tea cosy on page 128. Try to decorate the various hearts with different threads and movements when fastening them.
- Finish the hanging with a binding.

Square Pot Holders

7¾ x 7¾in (19.5 x 19.5cm)

Stitch as follows for two pot holders:

- Cut out two squares in light fabrics, 6 x 6in (15.25 x 15.25cm), eight squares in red-checked fabric, 1½ x 1½in (4 x 4cm) and eight red rectangles, 1½ x 6in (4 x 15.25cm).
- Sew the various pieces together for the two pot holders following the layout shown in the photograph above.

- Quilt on batting (wadding) and a nice fabric for the backing, using gently curved lines.
- Sew a red binding on to both pot holders and sew on hanging loops with buttons.
- Appliqué on the heart (pattern on page 152). Machine sew two or three straight seams around the heart, about ⅛in (3mm) from the raw edges, sewing freehand. This will give you a visible raw edge around the entire heart and visible appliqué seams on the back of the pot holder.

Christmas Runner and Cushions

Christmas Cushions

Stitch as follows:

- All three cushions shown here have borders of the same width surrounding the centre piece: 3½in (9cm), with seam allowance. The corner squares are 3½ × 3½in (9 × 9cm) and all the small squares are 1½ × 1½in (4 × 4cm), including seam allowances.
- Sew the small squares together to blocks made up of nine pieces, as shown in the photograph. (See page 118 for the layout of the top cushion shown in the large photograph opposite.)
- For the heart cushion, attach the appliqué hearts (pattern on page 152) at the end, as for the pot holders on page 130, on the centre piece, which is 8½ × 8½in (21.5 × 21.5cm).
- Machine quilt the cushions with a straight seam in gently curved lines and sew on a closing mechanism, for instance buttons, when sewing on a binding.

Christmas Runner

12 × 23in (30.5 × 58.5cm)

Once you have made the three cushions, a matching runner would look great. You can use the same nine-patch blocks as for the cushions – the patches are 3½ × 3½in (9 × 9cm) including seam allowance – and connect them with strips measuring 3½ × 6in (9 × 15.25cm). The sets of strips are sewn out of three strips, each 1½ × 6in (4 × 15.25cm). The light squares in the centre are 6 × 6in (15.25 × 15.25cm).

Ice-Blue Bedspread

60 × 80in (152 × 203cm)

This bedspread uses the same block as in the Christmas throw on page 123 and the same stitching procedure. With slightly different measurements and colours, this is how the bedspread will look. The new measurements for the squares are 3 x 3in (7.5 x 7.5cm). The blocks' new measurements are 10 x 10in (25.5 x 25.5cm) and the bedspread is made up of eight horizontal rows of six blocks. The new colours are light and medium blue and white against light blue/beige.

White as Snow Runner

10½ × 35½in (26.5 × 90cm)

You will sew this simple runner made of squares in no time at all, so why not make lots of different ones – red, blue, yellow, purple, green and so on – and you will have runners for all seasons and occasions. Maybe you will even have a spare one you can give away.

Stitch as follows:

The runner is created from forty-two white squares and fourteen beige squares, each 3 × 3in (7.5 × 7.5cm). Look at the picture on the left and arrange the squares in fourteen horizontal rows of four squares each. For the two centre rows, every other square is white and beige. The two outer rows are white.

Once the squares have been stitched together simply machine quilt the whole runner, with batting and backing, with simple straight seams and add a beige print binding to finish it all off.

Christmas Red

Brighten up your décor at Christmas time with festive reds and creams. The tablecloth is easy to make and could have matching place mats too. The elves wall hanging and mini quilt (overleaf) feature appliqué and are great fun.

Christmas Tablecloth
25½ × 25½in (65 × 65cm)

I sewed this tablecloth from squares, 3 × 3in (7.5 × 7.5cm), using red, dark brown and light fabrics. They are arranged so there are large red squares surrounded by a network of light and brown squares. I machine quilted the tablecloth diagonally.

Elves Wall Hanging
14¼ × 15in (36 × 38cm)

Can you see the Christmas elves on the wall? They are appliqués on a background that is red and checked, 3½ × 15in (9 × 38cm) and a light fabric with red writing, which is 11¼ × 15in (28.5 × 38cm). I have fastened the elves in place with a machine seam and blanket stitches. The round noses are sewn on by hand, with a tiny amount of batting (wadding) inside. I free-motion quilted the wall hanging. The pattern for the elves is on page 152 – all three have the same beard but different hats. The left one is number 1, the centre one number 2 and the right-hand one is number 3.

Elves Mini Quilt

3⅛ x 5⅛in (8 x 13cm)

I made the elves a mini quilt as a present, which was hung on the wall at once. It has a centre piece made up of four blocks, each made up of four squares, 1 x 1in (2.5 x 2.5cm). I sewed a square, 1½ x 1½in (4 x 4cm), on to the sides of the four-square blocks and also in between them. I then had to cut the block to size to get a set of blocks standing on edge. Cut the seam allowance to half the width along all the seams you have sewn. This will make it easier to sew the hanging together.

There is a border 1½in (4cm) wide along two of the sides. Cut out the backing and quilt the hanging by hand with small stitches and thin batting (wadding). Attach an edging. Fasten the quilt with a few small stitches to the elves wall hanging.

Patterns and Diagrams

Descending
Angels
(page 58)

142

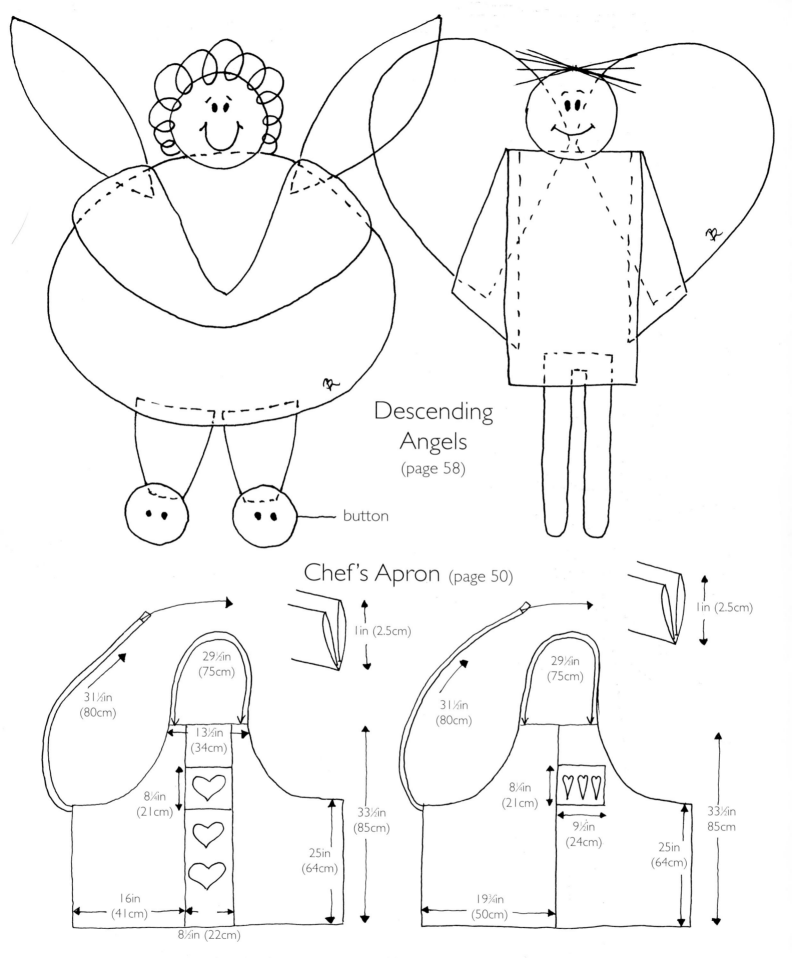

Descending
Angels
(page 58)

button

Chef's Apron (page 50)

1in (2.5cm)

1in (2.5cm)

31½in
(80cm)

29½in
(75cm)

13½in
(34cm)

8¼in
(21cm)

33½in
(85cm)

25in
(64cm)

16in
(41cm)

8½in (22cm)

31½in
(80cm)

29½in
(75cm)

8¼in
(21cm)

9½in
(24cm)

33½in
85cm

25in
(64cm)

19¾in
(50cm)

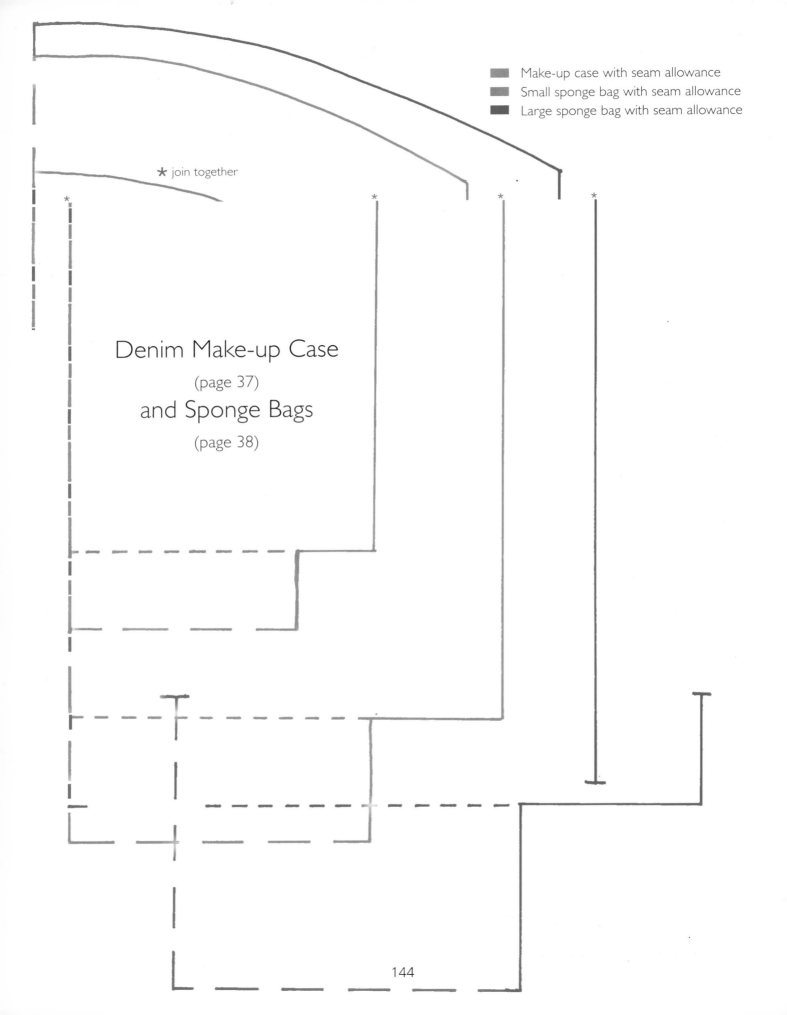

Make-up case with seam allowance
Small sponge bag with seam allowance
Large sponge bag with seam allowance

★ join together

Denim Make-up Case
(page 37)
and Sponge Bags
(page 38)

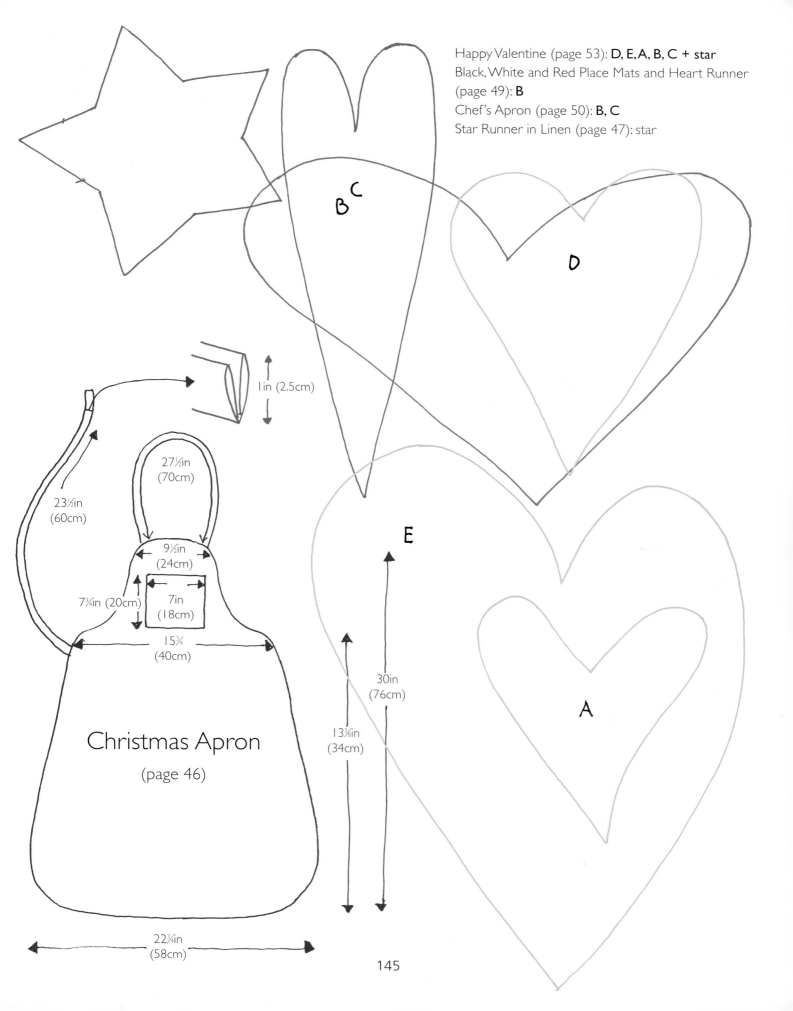

Happy Valentine (page 53): **D, E, A, B, C + star**
Black, White and Red Place Mats and Heart Runner
(page 49): **B**
Chef's Apron (page 50): **B, C**
Star Runner in Linen (page 47): star

B ^C

D

E

A

1in (2.5cm)

27½in
(70cm)

23½in
(60cm)

9½in
(24cm)

7¾in (20cm)

7in
(18cm)

15¾
(40cm)

30in
(76cm)

13⅜in
(34cm)

Christmas Apron

(page 46)

22¾in
(58cm)

145

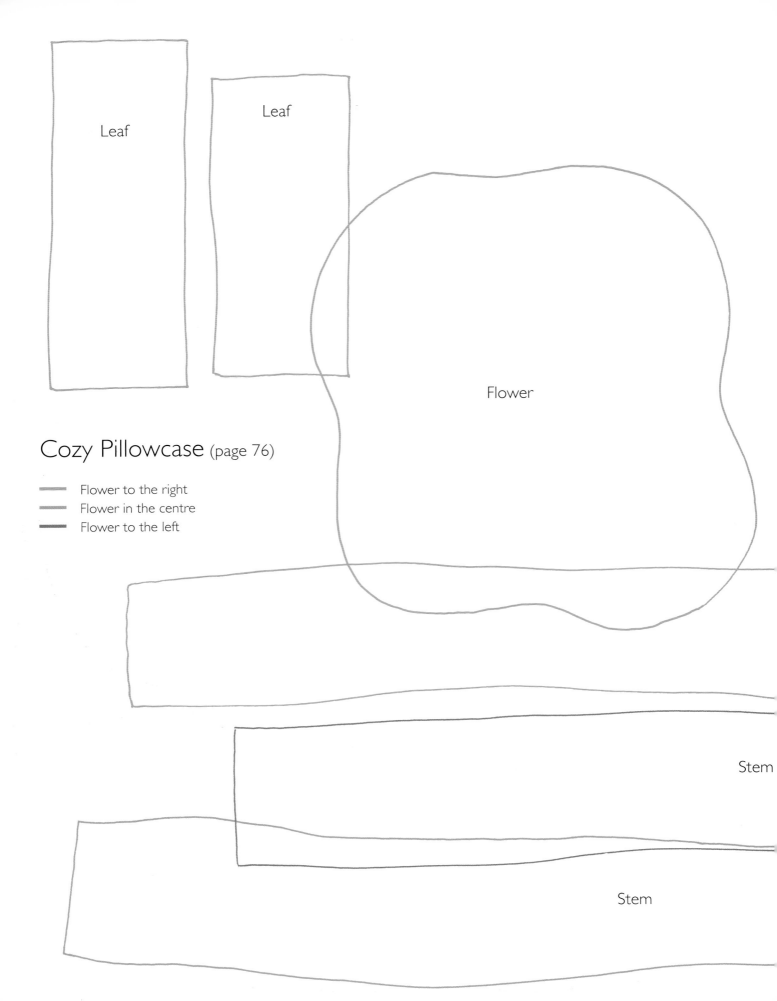

Leaf

Leaf

Flower

Cozy Pillowcase (page 76)

▬▬ Flower to the right
▬▬ Flower in the centre
▬▬ Flower to the left

Stem

Stem

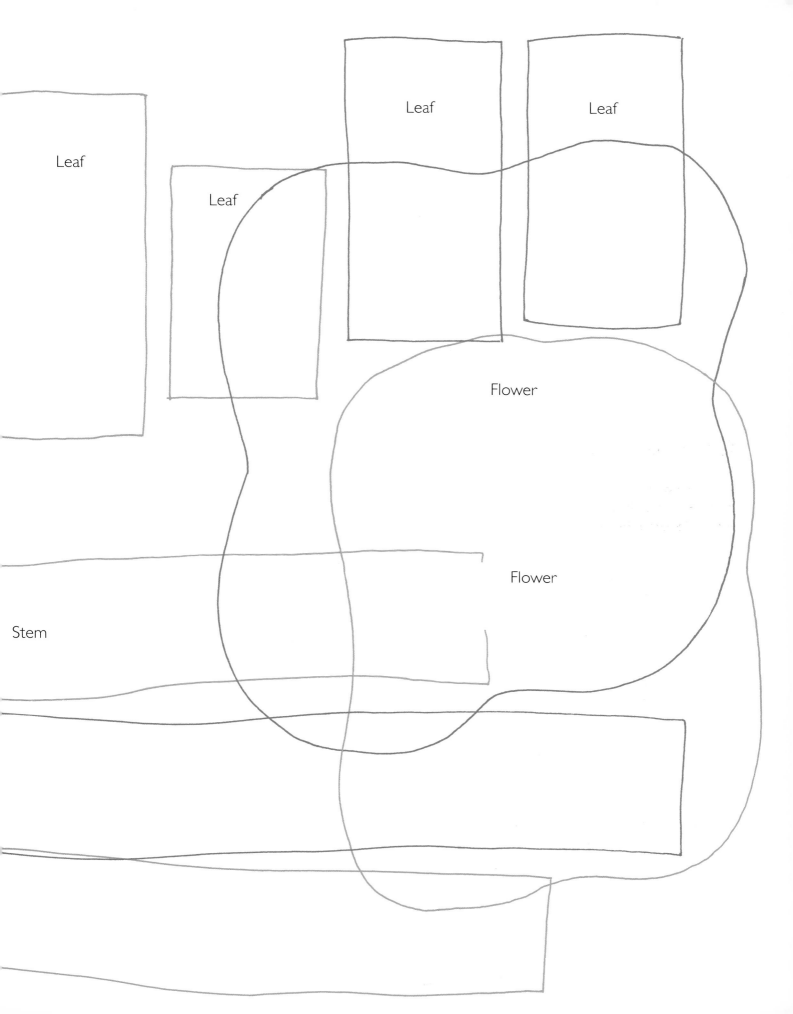

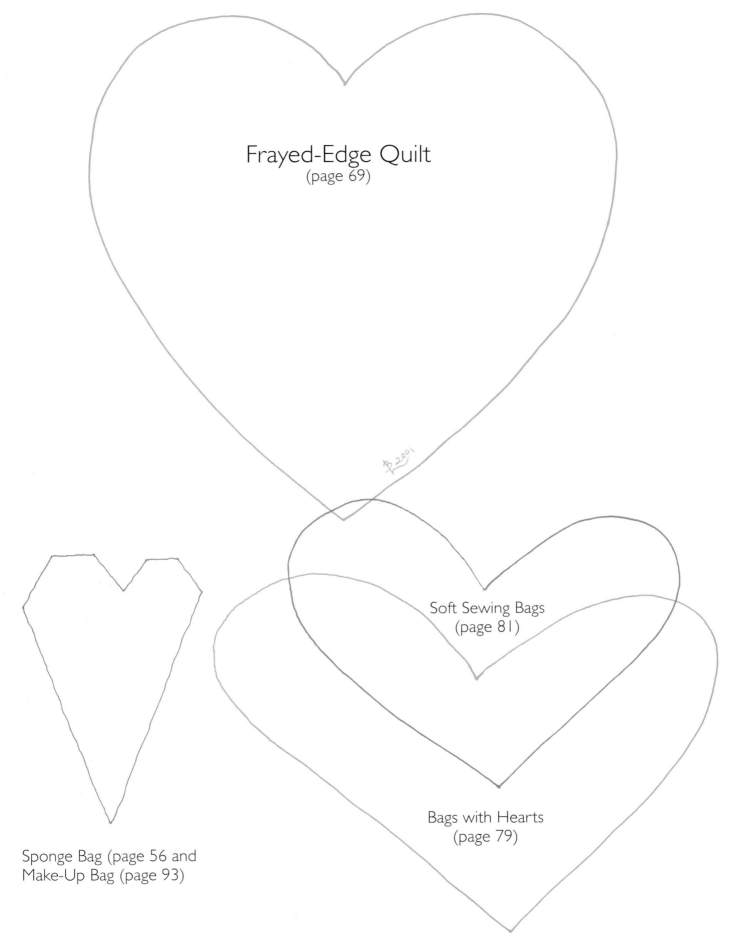

Frayed-Edge Quilt
(page 69)

Soft Sewing Bags
(page 81)

Bags with Hearts
(page 79)

Sponge Bag (page 56 and
Make-Up Bag (page 93)

Bite of Autumn Throw

(page 96)

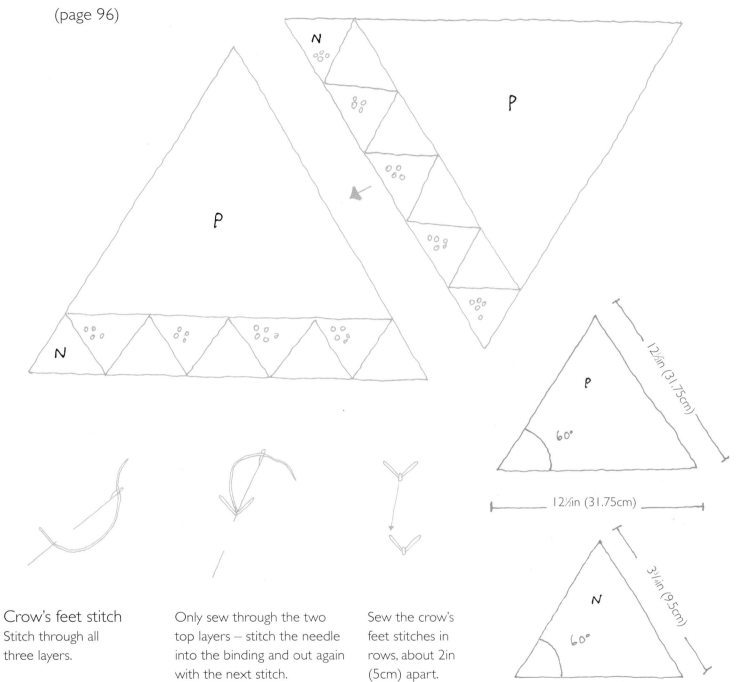

Crow's feet stitch
Stitch through all three layers.

Only sew through the two top layers – stitch the needle into the binding and out again with the next stitch.

Sew the crow's feet stitches in rows, about 2in (5cm) apart.

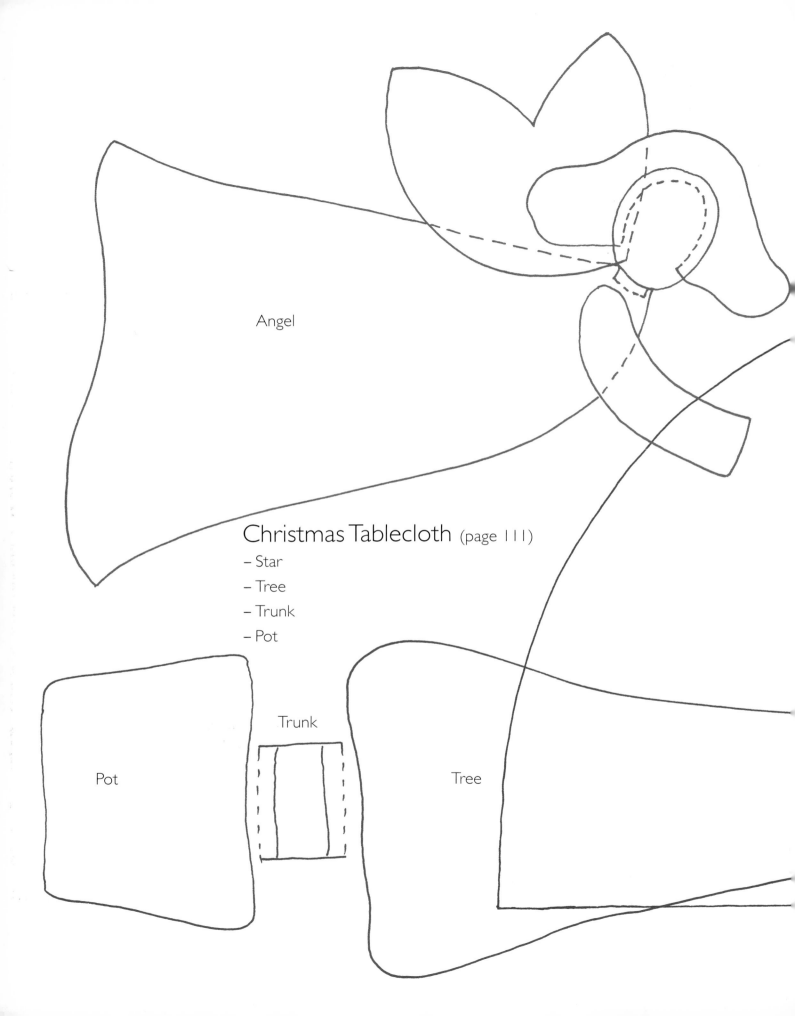

Angel

Christmas Tablecloth (page 111)

– Star
– Tree
– Trunk
– Pot

Pot

Trunk

Tree

Advent wall hanging (page 108)

– Large heart
– Small heart
– Star
– Angel

Mat with Hearts

– Small heart

Large heart

Small heart

Star

Tea Cosy (page 128) (with seam allowance included)

Fold here

Elves Wall Hanging (page 138)

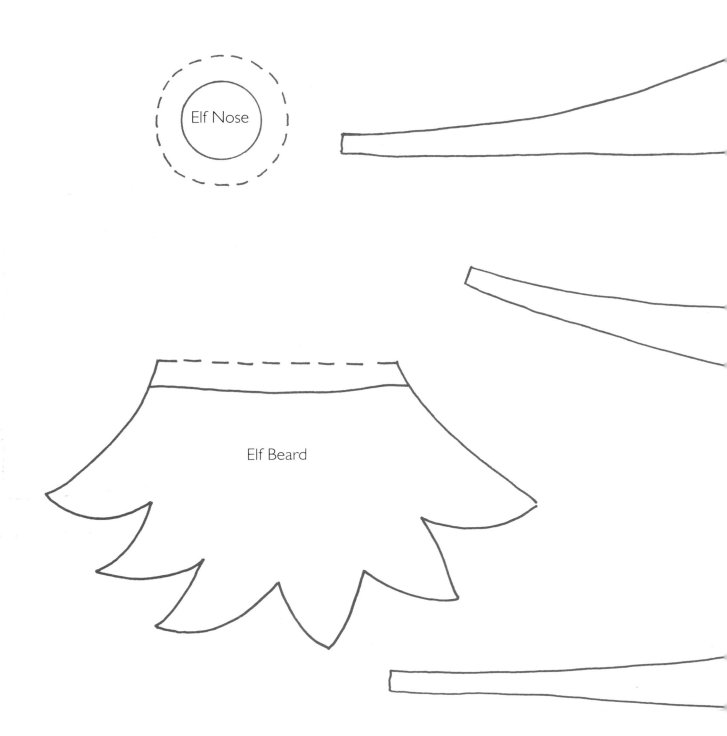

Elf Nose

Elf Beard

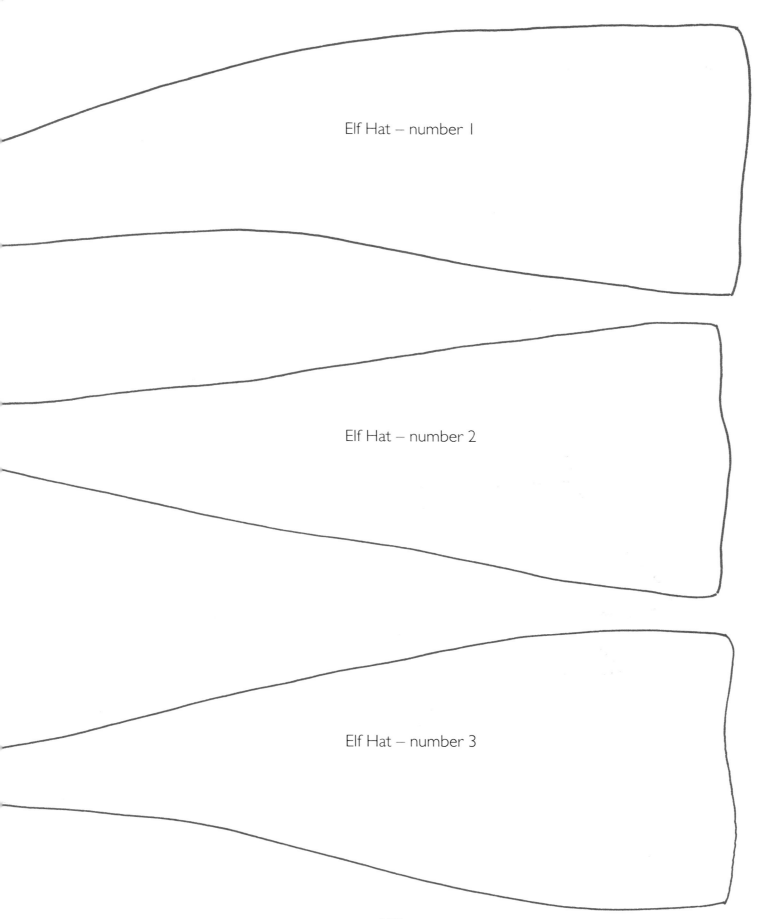

Elf Hat – number 1

Elf Hat – number 2

Elf Hat – number 3

Advent Celebration (page 107)

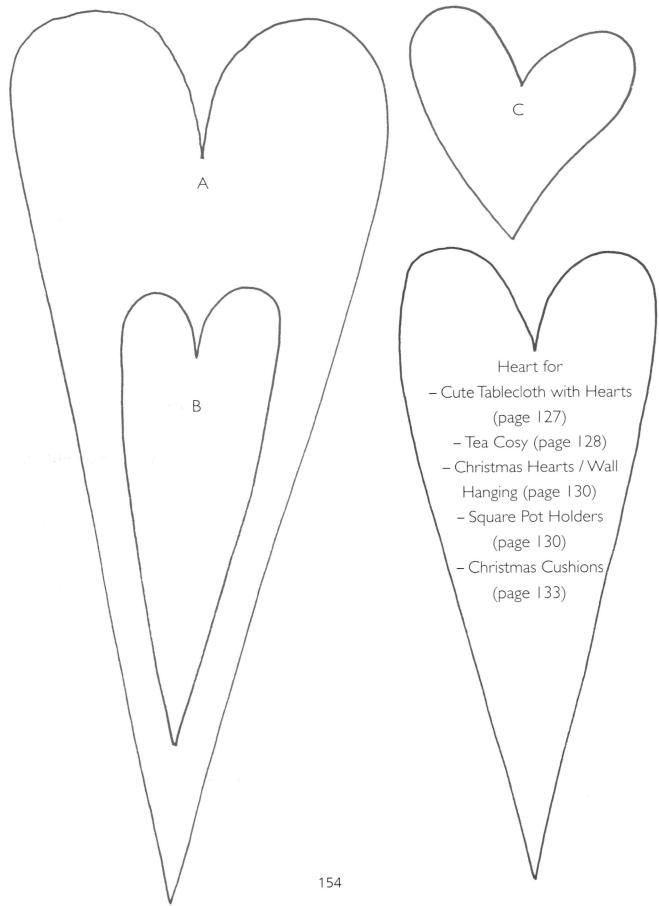

A

B

C

Heart for
– Cute Tablecloth with Hearts
(page 127)
– Tea Cosy (page 128)
– Christmas Hearts / Wall
Hanging (page 130)
– Square Pot Holders
(page 130)
– Christmas Cushions
(page 133)

Quilting Suppliers

If contacting suppliers by post, remember to include a stamped, self-addressed envelope.

The Bramble Patch
West Street, Weedon, Northants NN7 4QU, UK
tel: 01327 342212
For general quilting supplies

Coats Crafts UK
PO Box 22, Lingfield House, Lingfield Point,
McMullen Road, Darlington,
County Durham DL1 1YQ, UK
tel: 01325 394237 (consumer helpline)
www.coatscrafts.co.uk
For Anchor stranded cotton (floss) and other embroidery threads

Coats and Clark USA
PO Box 12229, Greenville, SC 29612-0229
Tel: (800) 648 1479
www.coatsandclark.com

The Cotton Patch
1285 Stratford Road, Hall Green, Birmingham B28 9AJ, UK
tel: 0121 702 2840
web: www.cottonpatch.net
For general quilting supplies

DMC Creative World
Pullman Road, Wigston, Leicestershire LE18 2DY, UK
tel: 0116 281 1040
fax: 0116 281 3592
web: www.dmc/cw.com
For stranded cotton (floss), perlé cotton and other embroidery threads

Kreinik Manufacturing Company Inc
3106 Timanus Lane, Suite 101, Baltimore, MD 21244 USA
tel: 1800 537 2166
email: kreinik@kreinik.com
web: www.kreinik.com
For a wide range of metallic threads

Madeira Threads (UK) Ltd
PO Box 6
Thirsk
North Yorkshire YO7 3BX
Tel: 01845 524880
E-mail: acts@madeira
Website: www.madeira.co.uk
(mail order)

Madeira (USA) Ltd
PO Box 6068, 30 Bayside Court, Laconia, NH 03246, USA
tel: 603 528 4264
For Madeira threads

The Quilt Room
20 West Street, Dorking,
Surrey RH4 1BL, UK
tel: 01306 877307
web: www.quiltroom.co.uk
For general quilting supplies

Ragbags
Coney Garth, 3 Kirkby Road, Ripon, North Yorks HG6 2EY, UK
tel: 01845 526047
web: www.ragbags.net
For recycled fabrics

The Silk Route
Cross Cottage, Cross Lane, Frimley Green, Surrey GU16 6LN, UK
tel: 01252 835781
web: www.thesilkroute.co.uk
For silk fabrics, threads and ribbons

Index